T0305969

EMPLOYMENT

Employment: A Key Idea for Business and Society introduces a topic that many of us take for granted yet is central to how we understand business and management. Most people work for the majority of their lives and, in recent years, employment has become a topic of popular debate, particularly asking what the future of work could be. Much of this has focused on the role of technology and automation, as well as the growth of the gig economy and new forms of work.

This book provides new ways to think about our own experiences of work and debates on employment. The book covers the history of employment, key changes to work, and a global perspective. The major debates in employment are introduced, providing theories for readers to develop their own perspectives. In particular, the book reappraises management theory, the role of workers' agency in changing work, surveys the state of current research and methods, and sketches out the key changes on the horizon for employment.

This book will provide students with a critical introduction to employment, equipping them with the resources to research, understand, and rethink the topic.

Dr Jamie Woodcock is a senior lecturer at the University of Essex and a researcher based in London. He is the author of *The Fight Against Platform Capitalism* (University of Westminster Press, 2021), *The Gig Economy* (Polity, 2019), *Marx at the Arcade* (Haymarket, 2019), and *Working the Phones* (Pluto, 2017). His research is inspired by workers' inquiry and focuses on labour, work, the gig economy, platforms, resistance, organising, and video games. He is on the editorial board of *Notes from Below* and *Historical Materialism*.

KEY IDEAS IN BUSINESS AND MANAGEMENT
Edited by Stewart Clegg

Understanding how business affects and is affected by the wider world is a challenge made more difficult by the disaggregation between various disciplines, from operations research to corporate governance. This series features concise books that break out from disciplinary silos to facilitate understanding by analysing key ideas that shape and influence business, organizations and management.

Each book focuses on a key idea, locating it in relation to other fields, facilitating deeper understanding of its applications and meanings, and providing critical discussion of the contribution of relevant authors and thinkers. The books provide students and scholars with thought-provoking insights that aid the study and research of business and management.

Bureaucracy
A Key Idea for Business and Society
Tom Vine

Professions
A Key Idea for Business and Society
Mike Saks

Surveillance
A Key Idea for Business and Society
Graham Sewell

Sustainability
A Key Idea for Business and Society
Suzanne Benn, Melissa Edwards and Tim Williams

Human Rights
A Key Idea for Business and Society
Karin Buhmann

Complexity
A Key Idea for Business and Society
Chris Mowles

Power
A Key Idea for Business and Society
Reinoud Bosch

Employment
A Key Idea for Business and Society
Jamie Woodcock

For more information about this series, please visit: www.routledge.com/Key-Ideas-in-Business-and-Management/book-series/KEYBUS

EMPLOYMENT

A Key Idea for Business and Society

Jamie Woodcock

Routledge
Taylor & Francis Group

LONDON AND NEW YORK

Designed cover image: © Getty Images

First published 2023
by Routledge
4 Park Square, Milton Park, Abingdon, Oxon OX14 4RN

and by Routledge
605 Third Avenue, New York, NY 10158

Routledge is an imprint of the Taylor & Francis Group, an informa business

British Library Cataloguing-in-Publication Data
A catalogue record for this book is available from the British Library

ISBN: 978-1-032-24728-1 (hbk)
ISBN: 978-1-032-24725-0 (pbk)
ISBN: 978-1-003-27990-7 (ebk)

DOI: 10.4324/9781003279907

Typeset in Bembo
by Newgen Publishing UK

CONTENTS

FIGURES

TABLES

ACKNOWLEDGEMENTS

This book is the culmination of research, teaching, and writing on the subject of employment across quite a few different universities and with a wide range of colleagues. Through discussions with other researchers, as well as students, my understanding of employment has been both shaped and challenged – and I hope this has found its way into the book. I would like to thank Terry Clague for commissioning the book and the rest of the team at Routledge for their support throughout the process. Finally, I would like to thank Lydia for her ongoing support in writing another book. You give me the strength to finish work projects and enjoy life outside of employment – as we all should be able to do.

INTRODUCTION

What is Employment and Why Does it Matter?

Employment is a relationship between two parties in which a worker or employee agrees to work for an employer. The relationship is regulated by a contract, whether written, verbal, formal, or informal. At the most basic level, the employee or worker agrees to provide their labour to work for an employer or boss, who pays them in return.

This book is part of the Key Ideas in Business and Management series and introduces a topic that many of us take for granted, yet is central to how we understand society, business, and management. Most of us will work in some way and it is an activity that we will likely do for the majority of our lives. We often think of employment as a natural part of life, providing an income and shaping how we interact with the world. In recent years, employment has become a topic of popular debate, particularly asking what the future of it could be. Much of this has focused on the role of technology and automation, as well as the growth of the gig economy and new forms of work.

The aim of this book is to provide new ways to think about our own experiences of work and debates on employment. It will develop a critical approach to understanding of employment, starting from the perspective of people in work. Across the chapters, the book covers the history of employment, key changes to work, and introduces a global perspective. The major debates in employment are introduced, providing critical resources and theories for readers to develop their own perspectives. In particular, the book reappraises management theory, the role of workers' agency in changing work, surveys the state of current research and methods, and sketches out the key changes on the horizon for employment. It therefore aims to provide a critical introduction to employment, equipping readers with the resources to research, understand, and rethink the topic.

Chapter one discusses a critical history of employment. It starts by looking at the beginnings of work and how the relations formed that would go on to become what we now understand as employment. In particular, this history focuses on the birth of capitalism and the industrial revolution as a key moment. It then moves on to examine the role of exploitation at work, exploring this through both Taylor's scientific management and labour process theory. The next part surveys how struggles over employment have shaped the relationship, before concluding with how this history relates to employment today.

In chapter two, the analysis steps back to discuss the global division of labour. This starts by examining statistics on different kinds of employment across the world. The chapter introduces the concept of imperialism to make sense of the continuing global inequalities and patterns of extraction from the Global South to the Global North. It then moves on to discuss the role of unemployment and the different forms this can take, as well as considering informal work and unpaid labour. The chapter concludes by reflecting on global differences and how they can help to make sense of employment.

Chapter three focuses on the issue of managing employment. It introduces the need for, and importance of, management in the employment relationship. In order to address this, a brief history of management is considered, before moving on to consider some key parts of the management process. First, before employment with recruitment and selection; second, during employment with pay and rewards; and third, to prevent or mitigate the end of employment with retention and turnover. The chapter concludes by reflecting on the role of workers within this process and considers how management is implemented in practice.

For chapter four, the book moves to discuss a series of key themes and dynamics that are reshaping employment. First, it examines state regulation and employment rights; second, the public sector and the state as employer; third, post-industrial employment and service work; fourth, emotional and affective labour; fifth, precarious work; sixth, platforms and the gig economy; and seventh, trade union decline and renewal. Each of these topics are considered in relation to the changes they involve for employment, as well as featuring both examples and literature from the field.

Chapter five of the book moves on to discuss researching employment. Throughout this chapter practical examples of how to conduct research are discussed, both in terms of academic research, but also with how these could be useful in employment itself. It starts with a brief history of research in the area. The next parts consider what kind of research questions can be asked and how to ensure ethics in research. The chapter then details different methods: first, collecting data and quantitative research; second, interviews; and third, ethnography. It concludes by reflecting on why research on employment is important today.

Chapter six concludes the book. It provides a reflection on the different possible futures of work and employment, noting some of the key changes that have been discussed so far. The chapter also provides a series of academic exercises that can be used by students or those interested in experimenting and thinking about employment.

WHAT IS EMPLOYMENT?

Employment is a practice that seems so embedded in our lives. We often get asked (and may dread) the question, 'So what do you do?' at awkward social occasions. The idea that we need to tell others what we are employed to do so they can judge us is deeply ingrained in much culture. Work is the activity that we will spend most of our lives doing. It shapes how we interact with the world and each other, as well as structuring our relationships to money, resources, power, and capital. Beyond this, it is through work that our needs are met and society is both made and constantly remade every day. As Philip Levine wrote in the poem, *What Work Is* (Levine, 1992):

> We stand in the rain in a long line
> waiting at Ford Highland Park. For work.
> You know what work is – if you're
> old enough to read this you know what
> work is, although you may not do it...

Studs Terkel, reflecting at the start of the collection *Working: People Talk About What They Do All Day and How They Feel About What They Do*, explains that work:

> is, by its very nature, about violence – to the spirit as well as to the body. It is about ulcers as well as accidents, about shouting matches as well as fistfights, about nervous breakdowns as well as kicking the doc around ... it is about a search, too, for daily bread, for recognition as well as cash, for astonishment rather than torpor; in short, for a sort of life rather than a Monday through Friday sort of dying.
>
> (Terkel, 2011, 1)

Employment can also be a huge source of opportunity. Employment provides regular pay, a way to access resources, and improve quality of life. For many people, employment can give a sense of identity. This is particularly the case for professional employment, in which workers can identify strongly with the culture of the work. For example, lawyer, doctors, or even academics. Through different kinds of work, we can learn many new skills and take on new challenges. Employment brings us into contact with people we may not otherwise have met, opening up access to new communities beyond our existing social circles. For some people, work can also give meaning to life, allowing people a way to pursue purpose beyond just themselves.

As the book will unpack and interrogate, there are a wide range of different experiences of employment, including positive, negative, and much in between. You may have a direct experience of what Levine and Terkel were discussing – or have very different experiences or expectations of employment. Before moving on to this, it is also worth noting the differences in terminology when discussing the topic. There is often a blending of three terms: labour, work, and employment. Labour comes from '*laborem*' meaning 'toil, hardship, and pain', while the etymological roots of work are '*wyrcan*', meaning creating something and '*wircan*' to affect something (Fuchs, 2016, 29). In some languages, like German, the two words can be translated into '*arbeit*', but in English they remain distinct although the meanings have changed. Today, we can think of how labour has come to mean the way we interact with the world. For example, labour 'is, in the first place, a process in which both man and Nature participate, and in which man of his own accord starts, regulates, and controls the material re-actions between himself and Nature' (Marx, 1867, 283). Work, on the other hand, has come to take on the more negative connotations of labouring: take, for example, the phrase 'I have to get up for work in the morning'. However, work and employment do not always overlap. There is much work that is unpaid, like domestic work (Dalla Costa and James, 1971), as well as being both gendered and racialised (Davis, 1982).

Employment may well involve labour and work but is more than that as a category. Employment is specifically paid work, and this gives it distinctive characteristics. If our ability to act upon the world is labour, then employment involves selling this labour-power to an employer. This is a peculiar phenomenon that lies at the heart of employment: the buying and selling of people's time. The process of employing someone – that is, the buying of the labour-power and then putting it to work – is an indeterminate process. Employment involves agreeing to complete work for someone else, giving over our time, whether that be for an hourly wage, an annual salary, or being paid for each task. It is complicated in practice by the differences in interests of workers (those selling their labour-power) and employers (those buying other people's labour-power). It raises important questions about how we work, why we work, who we work for, what we do when we work, and so on. It draws attention to the relationships between economic, politics, and society more widely.

The contractual relationship of employment has become much more complicated over time, developing far beyond someone saying they will pay someone else to do something. In the UK, for example, an 'employee' is defined in the Employment Rights Act 1996. Section 230 starts by noting that:

(1) In this Act 'employee' means an individual who has entered into or works under (or, where the employment has ceased, worked under) a contract of employment.

(2) In this Act 'contract of employment' means a contract of service or apprenticeship, whether express or implied, and (if it is express) whether oral or in writing.

(3) In this Act 'worker' (except in the phrases 'shop worker' and 'betting worker') means an individual who has entered into or works under (or, where the employment has ceased, worked under)—

   (a) a contract of employment, or

   (b) any other contract, whether express or implied and (if it is express) whether oral or in writing, whereby the individual undertakes to do or perform personally any work or services for another party to the contract whose status is not by virtue of the contract that of a client or customer of any profession or business undertaking carried on by the individual;

and any reference to a worker's contract shall be construed accordingly.

(4) In this Act 'employer', in relation to an employee or a worker, means the person by whom the employee or worker is (or, where the employment has ceased, was) employed.

(5) In this Act 'employment'—

    (a) in relation to an employee, means (except for the purposes of section 171) employment under a contract of employment, and

    (b) in relation to a worker, means employment under his contract;

and 'employed' shall be construed accordingly.

This definition starts with an employee entering into an agreement (a 'contract of employment') with an employer. The contract can be formally written down or expressed verbally. It might be clear or implied. What is important is that the relationship involves an individual working for another person or organisation.

From a simple starting point, employment has become a much more complicated phenomenon, often governed by specific legislation and regulations, as well as economic, political, and cultural expectations. For example, in the UK the full Act includes legislation that covers a wider range of aspects of employment, including: employment particulars, protection of wages, guarantee payments, Sunday working for shop and betting workers, protection from suffering detriment in employment, time off work, suspension from work, maternity and paternity, flexible working, termination of employment, unfair dismissal, redundancy payments, insolvency of employers.

In the UK, there is a legal distinction between an employee and a worker, something that does not exist in many other jurisdictions. For the purposes of this book (apart from the discussion of bogus self-employment later on) the two are used relatively interchangeably. The book also focuses, as the use of the employment law example suggests, on Britain. Chapter two takes a global view of employment and there are examples included throughout the book that widen the scope. However, the primary focus is on Britain, as this is where the author is based and the location of most of their research. The concept of imperialism is specifically discussed in chapter two, as well as consideration of the role in Britain in shaping and reshaping employment beyond its own borders.

Research on employment matters. It is important because too often employment is missing from the analysis of either history or the contemporary world. As Berthold Brecht puts it in the poem *A Worker Reads History*:

> Who built the seven gates of Thebes?
> The books are filled with names of kings.
> Was it the kings who hauled the craggy blocks of stone?
> And Babylon, so many times destroyed.
> Who built the city up each time? In which of Lima's houses,
> That city glittering with gold, lived those who built it?
> In the evening when the Chinese wall was finished
> Where did the masons go? Imperial Rome
> Is full of arcs of triumph. Who reared them up? Over whom
> Did the Caesars triumph? Byzantium lives in song.
> Were all her dwellings palaces? And even in Atlantis of the legend
> The night the seas rushed in,
> The drowning men still bellowed for their slaves.

We sometimes think of history as the creation of great men (and sometimes women) who through sheer will transformed the world around them. We think less of the day-to-day activities that Brecht notes that created the conditions in which these leaders could act. Employment often slides into the background of how we make sense of the world. News stories are filled with world leaders, global politics, and increasingly crises that will shape our future.

The aim of this book is to introduce the ideas, concepts, and methods that can inspire a fresh look at employment. Whether that is to better make sense of your studies, future work, or to imagine a different kind of world.

REFERENCES

Dalla Costa, M. and James, S. (1971) *The Power of Women and the Subversion of the Community*, Brooklyn, NY, Pétroleuse Press.

Davis, A.Y. (1982) *Women, Race and Class*, London, The Women's Press.

Fuchs, C. (2016) *Reading Marx in the Information Age: A Media and Communication Studies Perspective on Capital*, Abingdon, Routledge, vol. 1.

Levine, P. (1992) *What work is: poems*, New York, Knopf.

Marx, K. (1867) *Capital: A Critique of Political Economy* Vol. 1, 1976, London, Penguin Books.

Terkel, S. (2011) *Working: People Talk About What They Do All Day And How They Feel About What They Do*, New York, The New Press.

CHAPTER 1

A CRITICAL HISTORY OF EMPLOYMENT

To make sense of contemporary employment, it is first necessary to step back from the complexities of today and consider the historical roots of employment. This history of employment is part of a longer history about the different ways of organising work and how society structures the activities that people do.

Although it can often be harder to see today when looking at the complex relationships that spread across the world, at the core this is about we survive, both as people and as a society. Through work, society is made and remade every day. Think, for example, about all the different kinds of work that have been necessary for your day. This might involve the work that went into growing, preparing, and shipping the food and drinks you have consumed. The creation and maintenance of the building you are in. The clothes, smartphone, computer, and so on. Many of these involved complex webs of interrelated forms of work and employment. While we could survive for quite some time without these, some of these activities are needed each day.

This chapter will start by tracing out the longer history of how people have met their needs – or had their needs met – through labour and work. This will identify the broader shifts in production that have changed how people work, including the start of the employment relationship. The next section discusses the industrial revolution, considering the impact this had on employment. It then moves on to discuss the issue of exploitation at work and introduces labour process theory. Following this, the chapter discusses the struggles over employment that have shaped its form. It finishes by discussing how this helps us to make sense of the employment relationship today.

THE BEGINNINGS OF WORK

Since the beginning of human history, people have survived by using their labour to interact with the world. People constructed shelters, gathered food, hunted, made tools and so on. This is one of the unique aspects of human labour. As Hannah Arendt has argued, there is an important difference here, that 'labor is the activity which corresponds to the biological process of the human body ... the human condition of labor is life itself' (Arendt, 1998, 7). Similarly, As Marx argued:

> Labour is, in the first place, a process in which both man and Nature participate, and in which man of his own accord starts, regulates, and controls the material re-actions between himself and Nature. He opposes himself to Nature as one of her own forces, setting in motion arms and legs, head and hands, the natural forces of his body, in order to appropriate Nature's productions in a form adapted to his own wants. By thus acting on the external world and changing it, he at the same time changes his own nature. He develops his slumbering powers and compels them to act in obedience to his sway.
>
> (Marx, 1867, 283)

At the earliest stages, this involved trying to meet the most basic needs: food, shelter, care, and so on.

Starting from these basic activities, it is possible to sketch out a pre-history of employment based on the ways in which work has changed over time. One way to conceive of these historical shifts in work by considering changes to the mode of production. The mode of production is the way things are produced in society, which is a combination of the productive forces

DOI: 10.4324/9781003279907-2

(labour-power and the means of production – the tools, machinery, materials, technical knowledge, etc) and the relations of production (the sum of the relationships that people must enter in order to produce and survive). The mode of production therefore is a combination of what people produce and how they produce it (Marx and Engels, 1932). The first mode of production could therefore be identified as one of hunting and gathering.

While it may have looked a lot like work – and often hard work – this was not employment in the sense we would talk about it today. However, as David Graeber and David Wengrow note, 'most of human history is irreparably lost us. Our species, *Homo sapiens*, has existed for at least 200,000 years, but for most of that time we have next to no idea what was happening' (Graeber and Wengrow, 2021, i). This has not stopped many people making claims about what life was life then. For example, Hobbes claimed that people, in their natural state, had a life that was 'solitary, poor, nasty, brutish and short' (Hobbes, 2008, 84). Often these claims of the earlier period of human history become a foil for politics: either people are good or evil and the way we organise society should address that. They often also see previous ways of living as backward and the development of new forms of work and technology as progressive. However, rather than considering hunter-gatherer societies as living at or near subsistence levels, arguments have been put forward that their lives may have been relatively comfortable and secure (Sahlins, 2004). As Graeber and Wengrow unpack, the contemporary evidence points to a much more diverse and complex history (of what can be pieced together). They claim that while 'humans may not have begun their history in a state of primordial innocence, but they do appear to have begun it with a self-conscious aversion to being told what to do' (Graeber and Wengrow, 2021, 133).

This 'being told what to do' is a key part of employment. Subsistence living does not involve someone telling another what to do, but instead a person having to carry out labour in order to survive. As these activities developed and became more complex, work began to become organised in new ways. For example, fishing and capturing game required cooperation between members of a group. The advent of pottery, textiles, and metallurgy each involved greater specialisation. Agriculture changed the relationship of people to the land and each other. Clearly, there would have been forms of stratification that emerged with a division of labour, whether due to ability, age, or so on.

Class societies emerged around 5,000 years ago. Ruling minorities took control of what had previously been organised communally. Enforced through religion or royalty, this provided a layer of society with luxuries taken from production carried out by other people. The development of class society is often bound up with the second mode of production that is sometimes referred to as 'ancient' or slave society. It has been attributed to the rise of city states during the periods of Classical Greece and Rome, along with advances in toolmaking, written alphabet, and coinage. The development of the forces of production facilitated the emergence of city states, developing urban populations with new forms of social divisions. The new social relations involved property, and in particular the direct possession of other people through slavery: not only telling other people what to do but also owning them as property.

There is early evidence of work being given in exchange for pay. This would have required a few basic relations to be present. For example, a barter system that could facilitate that exchange, but also people who were organised with enough resources to become employers. There is evidence that the building of the pyramids in Egypt involved the setting up of encampments for workers. They were often paid in food and drink to undertake the work. In 1170 BC there was also the first recorded evidence of workers demanding something and refusing to work until this was met. Artisans 'attached to the royal tomb in the Valley of Kings repeatedly struck, complaining of inadequate or overdue rations and other irregularities' (Edgerton, 1951, 137). What is also interesting about this is that 'these were a very special group of men. They and their ancestors of some generations had lived in the same village in the Theban necropolis, made their tombs in a single locality, and maintained themselves principally by hewing and decorating the tombs of successive Pharaohs' (Edgerton, 1951, 137). While these workers may have been relying on the Pharaoh for rations, the Pharaoh relied on these workers in their pursuit of immortality after death.

The development of class society is an important change – particularly for the development of work. Class is a division that emerges in society. There can only be a ruling class because there is a subordinated class, and vice versa. Class is therefore relational and created through a relationship of domination between classes. However, these class societies did not last, instead they were transformed due to a combination of both internal and external pressures.

The collapse of the ancient mode of production led to a return to subsistence agriculture in much of Western Europe, sometimes called the 'Dark Ages'. This involved a return to people producing for their own need, rather than producing for someone else. However, a new form of organisation emerged in the 9th century: feudalism or the feudal mode of production. The fief was a key part of feudalism, which involves property rights that are inherited or granted from an overlord to a vassal. There may be, for example, a monarch, who grants rights over land to a series of lords, who each then grant rights to lower vassals. Each then hold those rights in fealty – that is, in return for feudal allegiance and service. An aristocratic class was developed, taking ownership over farmlands and the peasants who lived on the land. Peasants generally worked under a relationship of serfdom. This meant the peasants, or serfs, were required to work for the lord who owned the land. In return, they had limited rights to cultivate their own crops and had the right to protection from the lord. The relations of production were based on the exploitation of peasants by this new class of landowners, while peasants also worked for their own subsistence. This is also the origin of the term landlord that is still used today when renting property.

Given the time period and the scale of the area which is being referred to there was, of course, significant variation in the practical arrangements involved during feudalism. For the purposes of thinking about the history of work, what is important here is that the relationships of work did not involve workers who were free to choose who to work for, but instead mainly involved people working within dependent relationships who also had some autonomy. The next key change is to capitalism as the dominant mode of production and the new social relationships that came with it.

Often, the changes are considered as the move from backwards ways of working and organising society, towards more progressive and technologically developed activities. However, it is worth nothing that evidence is increasingly pointing towards the opposite. For example, David Graeber and David Wengrow have argued that:

> The average oppressed medieval serf still worked less than a modern nine-to-five office or factory worker, the hazelnut gatherers and cattle herders who dragged great slabs to build Stonehenge almost certainly worked, on average, less than that. It's only very recently that even the richest countries have begun to turn things around (obviously, most of us are not working as many hours as Victorian stevedores, though the overall decline in working hours is probably not as dramatic as we think). And for much of the world's population, things are still getting worse instead of better.
> (Graeber and Wengrow, 2021, 136)

It is possible therefore to understand not only the quality of work increasing (that is the formalisation, intensity, and regulation of it) over time, but also the quantity of it.

Regardless of the balance sheet of capitalism for society, there are a range of different opinions as to how and why capitalism came into being. For example, Max Weber wrote extensively about the birth of capitalism. In *The Protestant Ethic and the Spirit of Capitalism*, he makes an argument about the importance of the internalisation of a capitalist ideology (or spirit) that involves economic rationalisation in the pursuit of profit (Weber, 1930). Weber argued that this could particularly be found in Calvinism following the Protestant Reformation. In addition to the other dynamics (including waged work and the development of the market), he argued that there was a particular affinity between the Protestant religion and capitalism. Marx also notes this in his early writing, that:

> the cult of money has its asceticism, its self-denial, its self-sacrifice-economy and frugality, contempt for mundane, temporal and fleeting pleasures; the chase after the eternal treasure. Hence the connection between English Puritanism or Dutch Protestantism and money-making.
>
> (Marx, 1973, 232)

Indeed, later writers have argued that the development of capitalism in the 16th century increased the spread of English Calvinist Puritanism, rather than the other way round, as Weber claimed (Tawney, 1926).

The transition from feudalism to capitalism has long been an area of debate. Following the publication of *Studies in the Development of Capitalism* (Dobb, 1946), there have been arguments about the origins of capitalism – this is sometimes known as the 'transition debate' (Brenner, 1976; 1977; Anderson, 1974; Wallerstein, 1974). Parts of this literature have been critiqued as Eurocentric, focusing on the development of capitalism in Western Europe. While capitalism may have taken root in Europe, other parts of the world were as or more economically and culturally 'developed'. As Chris Harman has argued:

> The advance over millennia of the forces of production and the technologies and scientific knowledge associated with them is not a peculiar European phenomenon. Nor is the 'spirit of capitalism'. Capitalism is a product of world history, which for a brief historical period found a focus in the western fringes of Eurasia before going on to transform the whole world. As it did so, it created new relations of production, and with them new social forces driven to oppose it.
>
> (Harman, 2004)

Other perspectives argue for the importance of merchant capital more widely, rather than the focus on processes taking place in Europe (Banaji, 2020).

Whichever perspective is more convincing, at some point after the 14th century feudalism was supplanted by capitalism and these processes reached their peak with the Industrial Revolution from 1780–1850. This is about more than identifying a point in which capitalism 'started'. In terms of what this means for employment, Henry Heller summarises the stakes of this debate:

> In studying the transition from feudalism to capitalism we are trying to explain both theoretically and concretely the transition from the feudal mode to the capitalist. But to put it in more concrete terms, how, over the course of centuries, did the majority of people come to live in towns and cities rather than the countryside? How was it that whereas under feudalism most people were legally defined as serfs tied to a manor while paying rent in kind or cash to a landlord, many if not all producers in capitalism became economically and legally free producers working for wages and were conceived as such? How, finally did it come about that whereas the object of economic activity under feudalism was consumption, under capitalism it came to be the accumulation of profit? Understanding the means by which this transformation came about is the focus of the transition debate.
>
> (Heller, 2011, 13)

While the development of capitalism introduced a new social relationship that has become the basis of modern employment. This requires workers that are 'free in a double sense', free to work for whomever they choose, but freed from any other way to make a living than by working (Marx, 1867, 272). This is a condition that is shared by many people today: having to get a job in order to survive. However, the development of capitalism is also deeply intertwined with the use of another social relationship of work: slavery. Starting in the 16th century and lasting into the 19th century, the transatlantic slave trade involved European countries, including Portugal,

Britain, France, Spain, and the Netherlands, operating a triangular route. First, transporting goods from Europe to Africa. Second, enslaving people and forcibly transporting them from Africa to the Americas and the Caribbean. Third, returning the goods produced by slaves to Europe, including cotton, sugar, and tobacco. It is estimated that 12.5 million were enslaved and forced to work on plantations (Eltis and Richardson, 2015).

In the UK, the slave trade was hugely profitable, with cities like London, Bristol, Liverpool, and Glasgow centrally involved. It is still possible in each of these cities today to see the marks of slavery, either in the buildings that were paid for with the profits or in the names of buildings and roads that signal the connection. Slavery is sometimes referred to as an aberration in the development of work, disconnected from the development of employment more widely. In other accounts, slavery is understood as pre-capitalist (Genovese, 1988). However, Eric Williams argued that capitalism replaced slavery once the European ruling classes had accumulated enough capital from the slave trade that the industrial revolution could start (Williams, 1994). Slavery was therefore the foundation of the industrial revolution – and indeed the decline of slavery was not a moral question, but one of economics. This perspective has led to much debate, but has also been extended by later research that argues that much more than just the industrial revolution was shaped in Europe by the slave trade (Blackburn, 2010). It also was not only the profits of slavery that fuelled the industrial revolution, but also commodities produced by slavery, particularly sugar (Mintz, 1985).

In Europe, slavery was externalised to the transatlantic trade and the colonies, however, in North America it existed alongside other forms of employment. The ending of slavery shifted social relations and 'through the lens of contract many Americans conceptualized the transition from slavery to freedom and pondered the ambiguities of a culture that deplored the traffic in slaves while pushing nearly all else to sale in the free market' (Stanley, 1998, x). The continuing effect of slavery for employment is therefore tied to the contract, but also the international relations of imperialism, the extraction of wealth from most of the world to Europe and the Global North, as well as the continuing effects of inequality and racism within and across different societies.

THE INDUSTRIAL REVOLUTION

The transition to a capitalist mode of production reached a climax with the industrial revolution. The previous ways of organising work were gradually replaced with a new relationship that increasingly looked more like contemporary employment. This involves an important change in how human labour is treated. It becomes a commodity, like other resources used in production. This is different to a peasant spending time producing for themselves and then either giving some of the harvest or their time to a lord. It is different to slavery as the ability to work is not seized, along with the person themselves, and taken as the property of the slave owner. Instead, the worker is able to sell this commodity themselves. And indeed, has to sell this as they have no other means to survive. The basis of modern employment is the ability of people to sell their own labour-power to employers. For the time they are employed, they sell their time and effort to an employer, who then takes control to tell them what to do during that time.

This new class of people is sometimes called the working class. As Engels argued:

> The history of the proletariat begins with the second half of the last century, with the invention of the steam-engine and machinery for working cotton. These inventions gave rise, as is well known, to an industrial revolution, a revolution which altered the whole civil society; one, the historical importance of which is only now beginning to be recognised.
>
> (Engels, 1844, 15)

The industrial revolution is sometimes characterised as a process driven by technological innovations in machinery and the factory. At other points the large-scale transformations are presented, particularly the huge movement of people from the countryside and into the cities. However, when thinking about changes in work, it is important to remember the human effects that these changes had.

As E.P. Thompson argued:

> The process of industrialization is necessarily painful. It must involve the erosion of traditional patterns of life. But it was carried through with exceptional violence in Britain. It was unrelieved by any sense of national participation in communal effort, such as is found in countries undergoing a national revolution. Its ideology was that of the masters alone... The experience of immiseration came upon them in a hundred different forms; for the field labourer, the loss of his common rights and the vestiges of village democracy; for the artisan, the loss of his craftsman's status; for the weaver, the loss of livelihood and of independence; for the child, the loss of work and play in the home; for many groups of workers whose real earnings improved, the loss of security, leisure and the deterioration of the urban environment.
>
> (Thompson, 1991, 486)

The process of industrialisation therefore transformed much more than just the work process, reaching into and deeply affecting people's lives, as well as society. For example, E.P. Thompson noted that for the worker, 'his own share in the "benefits of economic progress" consisted in more potatoes, a few articles of cotton-clothing for his family, soap and candles, some tea and sugar, and a great many articles in the *Economic History Review*' (Thompson, 1991, 351). Workers became subjected to a new kind of discipline from becoming employed: the discipline of time, of having to wake up and work at particular times (Thompson, 1967). Often that meant very long working days. In the factory, conditions were dangerous. Legislation was introduced to try and curb some of the worst conditions in factories. The 1833 Factory Act introduced a series of changes aimed at children:

- Banning working at night
- Banning those under nine years old from working
- Limiting the working day to nine hours for those aged between 9–13 years
- Limiting the working day to twelve hours for those aged between 13–18 years
- Two hours schooling each day for those under 13
- The appointment of four factory inspectors to enforce the law

(UK Parliament, 2022)

The attempts at legislation like this give an impression of what conditions would have been like. While there had been previous Acts of parliament aiming to improve conditions, these lacked any enforcement mechanism. While this Act focused on children, the establishment of factory inspectors – albeit only four to oversee at least 4,000 mills – was a step forward. However, in practice the Act was widely evaded by most employers (UK Parliament, 2022).

Beyond the factory, the living conditions in industrial towns and cities was not much better. Overcrowding was common, as well as lack of amenities:

> This deterioration of the urban environment strikes us today, as it struck many contemporaries, as one of the most disastrous of the consequences of the Industrial Revolution, whether viewed in aesthetic terms, in terms of community amenities, or in terms of sanitation and density of population.
>
> (Thompson, 1991, 352)

The growth of factories was accompanied by the rapid urbanisation of people. Industrial cities quickly grew around these new factories to provide housing for workers. Manchester, for example, grew from a minor town to a major metropolis during the industrial revolution. The population increased from less than ten thousand to hundreds of thousands, drawing in workers from across Britain and Ireland. By the middle of the 19th century, half of the world output of cotton cloth was made by workers in Britain, yet no cotton was grown in the country at all. Instead, cotton was shipped into the newly developed cities like Manchester from ports in Liverpool, completing the triangular Atlantic slave trade. The damp weather in Manchester provided ideal conditions for storing cotton, before it would be transformed by factory workers into saleable goods.

Industrialisation introduced profound changes in work. Adam Smith, for example, argued that capitalism developed from individuals' desire to improve their own material circumstances (Smith, 1999a). For Smith, trade and exchange played a key role in doing this. Through trade, people were able to improve their own circumstances, moving from basic activities, through agriculture, and then commercialism. A key part of his argument was that as exchange develops and becomes more complex, there is an increasing specialisation and division of labour. Adam Smith explains the industrialisation of this process with the example of pin-making:

> To take an example, therefore, from a very trifling manufacture; but one in which the division of labour has been very often taken notice of, the trade of the pin-maker; a workman not educated to this business (which the division of labour has rendered a distinct trade), nor acquainted with the use of the same machinery employed in it (to the invention of which the same division of labour has probably given occasion), could scarce, perhaps, with his utmost industry, make one pin in a day, and certainly could not make twenty. But in the way in which this business is now carried on, not only the whole work is a peculiar trade, but it is divided into a number of branches, of which the greater part are likewise peculiar trades. One man draws out the wire, another straights it, a third cuts it, a fourth points it, a fifth grinds it at the top for receiving the head ... the important business of making a pin is, in this manner, divided into about eighteen distinct operations ... ten persons, therefore, could make among them upwards of forty-eight thousand pins a day. Each person, therefore, making a tenth part of forty-eight thousand pins, might be considered as making four thousand eight hundred pins in a day. But if they had all wrought separately and independently, and without any of them having been educated to this peculiar business, they could certainly not each of them have made twenty, perhaps not one pin in day.
>
> (Smith, 1999a, 109–110)

Factories, therefore, greatly increased the productivity of workers who were employed within them. This is the basis of the capitalist employment relationship. First, that unlike buying other commodities, the capitalist buys potential when they employ workers. Labour-power, as the capacity to work, can have varying outputs: one pin, 20, or 4,800 in Smith's example. By entering into employment, the 'labourer works under the control of the capitalist to whom his labour belongs; the capitalist taking good care that the work is done in a proper manner'. However, unlike the previous activities that workers may have undertaken, the result of that labour becomes 'the property of the capitalist and not that of the labourer, its immediate producer' (Marx, 1867, 291). The pin-makers do not own the pins that come out the other side of the process, instead receive a wage for their time worked. Through the 'purchase of labour-power, the capitalist incorporates labour, as a living agent of fermentation, into the lifeless constituents of the product' (Marx, 1867, 291). No matter how many materials are stacked up, the pin factory is useless without workers to carry out the different steps in the process of making pins.

Division of labour is often thought of as an incredibly important development in work. Most workers today do not have to know how to grow their own food, build shelter, make clothes, and so on. Instead, people can specialise to become teachers, nurses, train drivers, accountants, software engineers, and so on. Through specialisation – and the sharing of the results of that specialisation – it is possible to develop much more complex forms of employment. However, Adam Smith also warned of the risk of deep specialisation like that found in pin-making could have negative effects on those employed in it:

> The man whose whole life is spent in performing a few simple operations, of which the effects are perhaps always the same, or very nearly the same, has no occasion to exert his understanding or to exercise his invention in finding out expedients for removing difficulties which never occur. He naturally loses, therefore, the habit of such exertion, and generally becomes as stupid and ignorant as it is possible for a human creature to become.
>
> (Smith, 1999b, 368)

While the worker in the pin or cotton factory became significantly more productive, the conditions under which they worked did not markedly improve.

EXPLOITATION

One of the controversial topics relating to employment is exploitation. In the case of pin-making – and particularly with Adam Smith's explanation of the negative effects – it is clear to see the relationship of exploitation. Exploitation, at the core is an unfair relationship, in which one side benefits while the other loses out. It should be noted that 'due to this unfairness, exploitation is a highly emotive concept, involving value judgments from different perspectives' (Woodcock, 2020). Exploitation is frequently used in economics to refer to making use of resources, however exploitation in employment is often discussed in terms of extreme cases or those that require government intervention. These cases can be considered in terms of the 'transaction' being exploitative, rather than a 'structural' form of exploitation. Transactional exploitation may involve a particular worker being exploited by an unscrupulous boss, while structural exploitation involves one group taking advantage of another through the organisation of a system that is unfair (Sample, 2003).

The history of work discussed so far is one developed from a system that is structurally exploitative. One group – or class – employs another, both to their advantage and the disadvantage of workers. This exploitative relationship, that employers take the surplus from workers in production, is the foundation of employment. Marx and Engels famously argued that 'the history of all hitherto existing society is the history of class struggles' (Marx and Engels, 1848). The history covered in this chapter so far is cast as one riven with struggles between exploiters and exploited, covering the emergence of the first forms of ruling class, lords and peasants, and the birth of capitalism. Marx's premise for this understanding of capitalist employment is simple: that workers are paid less for their labour than the value of what they produce for the capitalist employer (Marx, 1867). Other classical liberal thinkers, like Locke or Hodgskin, connected these forms of exploitation to property rights. For example, that it is 'the right of individuals, to have and to own, for their own separate use and enjoyment, the produce of their own industry, with power freely to dispose of the whole of that in the manner most agreeable to themselves' (Hodgskin, 1832, 24).

The employment relationship is based on a social relationship in which workers must find employment to survive. Unlike peasants who could also work the land, workers – often through the process of enclosure of previously accessible lands – lost the ability to grow their own food for subsistence. Workers did not own the means of production – that is, the things used in the work process, whether factories, machineries, or tools – and so only had left their own labour-power to sell to employers to make a living. Capitalism, therefore, brings together two important actors: workers selling their labour-power and employers (or capitalists) who own the means of production but need people to work them. The organisation of the factory discussed above is only possible because it was owned by a capitalist who paid for it and could employ a large enough group of workers to make its operation profitable. The factory owner only employs workers to produce more with the machinery than it costs to employ them. Otherwise, it would not make sense for the capitalist who wants to turn a profit.

Marx was not alone in his understanding of labour-power as a commodity in production. He critically developed other classical economists like David Ricardo and Adam Smith. Marx, like Ricardo, argued that not only was labour-power a commodity, but it was a commodity that can produce value above its own cost. Thus, in the employment relationship, workers can produce more value than the cost of their wages. The difference – or what Marx called 'surplus value' – is appropriated as profit by capitalists (Marx, 1867, 320).

This is an important difference to other forms of production and exploitation that have been discussed in previous modes of production. Marx distinguishes between two ways that this exploitation can take place in practice. The first is increasing 'absolute surplus value'. This involves, for example, extending the working day. If workers are made to work longer each day, this increases how much they produce. This tactic emerges early in capitalism, seen with the incredibly long hours worked in the first factories. At this point, capitalists were only formally commanding workers in the factory. Later, 'relative surplus value' becomes more important as capitalists took control of the tools and organised these to control the workplace. This reduces the time necessary to complete tasks and greatly increases productivity – and therefore the exploitation of workers (Marx, 1867, 643).

Whether through absolute or relative approaches, exploitation is being intensified during the employment relationship. However, the term exploitation often comes with linguistic baggage. For example, often when the term exploitation is used it refers to an edge case of extreme behaviour, involving someone being taken advantage of – and often harmed in the process. The kind of exploitation being discussed here is a relationship of economic exploitation, which can also involve the other sense of exploitation, or it can be part of the daily experience of employment. There is also a benefit to people engaging in the employment relationship, even if it is structurally exploitative. For example, as Joan Robinson once argued, the 'misery of being exploited by capitalists is nothing compared to the misery of not being exploited at all' (Robinson, 1962, 45). The employment relationship provides a wage or salary which allows people to purchase the things they need to survive. Not entering this relationship (or having any other way to make money) is, as Robinson notes, an even worse situation to be in.

SCIENTIFIC MANAGEMENT

Many parts of the literature take this antagonistic relationship as a starting point for understanding employment. One of the most significant, and tied to this historical development discussed so far, is scientific management. Introduce by Frederick Winslow Taylor with the publication of *The Principles of Scientific Management* in 1911, it transformed both management theory and practice. For Taylor, 'management is the art of knowing what you want to do and then seeing that it is done in the best and cheapest way' (Taylor, 1967). This is a combination of both the absolute and relative intensification discuss above.

Taylor was arguably the first management consultant. He came from a wealthy family in the USA and had planned to study law at Harvard, but instead took up a machinist apprenticeship in the 1870s. This was, as Braverman has argued, 'extraordinary for anyone of his class', although he did start the 'craft apprenticeship in a firm whose owners were social acquaintances of his parents'

(Braverman, 1998, 70). Working on the shop floor, he developed a detailed understanding of the labour process in manufacturing. Following the apprenticeship, Taylor took up employment at the Midvale Steel Works, where he again had family connections. He was rapidly promoted, eventually becoming the director of research and the chief engineer. Taylor maintained his role as a foreman in the factory throughout.

During this time, Taylor developed a particular interest. He had noticed that workers in the factory would not necessarily work as hard as they could. This goes back to the issue of labour-power. Employers may employ people, but what they are purchasing is a potential, rather than a guarantee of how hard people will work. This became a major focus for Taylor:

> Underworking, that is, deliberately working slowly so as to avoid doing a full day's work, 'soldiering,' as it is called in this country, 'hanging it out,' as it is called in England, 'ca canae,' as it is called in Scotland is almost universal in industrial establishments, and prevails also to a large extent in the building trades ... this constitutes the greatest evil with which the working-people of both England and America are now afflicted.
>
> (Taylor, 1967, 13)

Clearly, Taylor saw this not only as a research problem, but also a major moral issue. His response was to undertake a sustained study of the labour process in factories. For *The Principles of Scientific Management*, Taylor set out to make three related arguments. First, that there was a great loss of inefficiency at work (the problem of soldiering). Second, to convince the reader that the solution to this inefficiency at work was scientific management. Third, that management can be a 'science', building upon clearly defined and provable laws, rules, and principles.

In order to build the argument for the book, Taylor developed a scientific approach for trying to understand each element of the work process. This was an attempt to replace informal methods in which workers held the knowledge for each step and managers did not. This meant that managers needed to take on 'the burden of gathering together all of the traditional knowledge which in the past has been possessed by the workmen and then the classifying, tabulating, and reducing this knowledge to rules, laws, and formulae' (Taylor, 1967, 36). It also meant using this scientific approach to select and train workers, rather than leaving the choice of work and training to workers themselves. Managers then needed to take a much more active role in ensuring that the work was being carried out in accordance with the scientific principles developed. This involves a shift in how factories were organised. Management should take over the work of planning, while workers should focus on carrying out the tasks. This is a division of labour between the planning and execution of the work.

There is a debate about how effective Taylorism was in practice. Taylor argued that:

> It is only through *enforced* standardization of methods, *enforced* adoption of the best implements and working conditions, and *enforced* cooperation that this faster work can be assured. And the duty of enforcing the adoption of standards and enforcing this cooperation rests with the *management* alone.
>
> (Taylor, 1967, 49)

From the employer's point of view, this was an expensive undertaking. In practice, 'very few firms adopted the proposal' and it was met with opposition from both employers and workers (Montgomery, 1987, 224). It meant disrupting the production process, spending time and money to study, standardise, and then reorganise the work. There may, instead, be smaller alterations that could be made alongside the work. The emphasis on speed could also lead to a deterioration of quality in output. It could also create new problems for management.

From the workers' point of view, it could be an exploitative process. Workers did not receive a larger share of the increased profits from efficiencies. Adam Smith's warning about increased specialisation and the monotony of tasks being broken down into simple steps became a reality for many workers. It is also important to understand what Taylor was trying to achieve:

> With the triumph of scientific management, unions would have nothing left to do, and they would have been cleansed of their most evil feature: the restriction of output. To underscore this idea, Taylor fashioned the myth that 'there has never been a strike of men working under scientific management', trying to give it credibility by constant repetition. In similar fashion he incessantly linked his proposals to shorter hours of work, without bothering to produce evidence of Taylorized firms that reduced working hours, and he revised his famous tale of Schmidt carrying pig iron at Bethlehem Steel at least three times, obscuring some aspects of his study and stressing others, so that each successive version made Schmidt's exertions more impressive, more voluntary and more rewarding to him than the last. Unlike Emerson, Taylor was not a charlatan, but his ideological message required the suppression of all evidence of worker's dissent, of coercion, or of any human motives or aspirations other than those his vision of progress could encompass. Workers' control, as machinists had exercised it, was simply castigated as 'soldiering', 'restriction of output,' a mindless abuse against the public interest.
>
> (Montgomery, 1987, 254)

Control was deliberately and explicitly being taken away from workers. The pace of work was greatly increased. Taylor, as the quote makes clear, was anti-trade union, meaning there was no room for bargaining over the changes. The increased efficiency and use of new machinery could also lead to unemployment as fewer workers would be needed. Moreover, many workers responded to changes in mass production by not turning up to work. Instead of soldiering, absenteeism became a problem for some managers as workers stopped turning up for work.

Despite these practical challenges, Taylorism represents an important shift, both in terms of theory and practice. It takes place at the turn of the 20th century, with the maturing of the employment relationship in industrial production. The industrial revolution created far-reaching changes for the lives of many people entering into employment relationships, including the disappearance of previous ways of living, the movement from the countryside into cities, working and living alongside large number of other workers, and doing new activities often over long days of work. Taylorism represents the next significant attempt to reorganise the labour process, changing the employment relationship once again.

LABOUR PROCESS THEORY

Taylor was, of course, not the only person interests in the labour process. People who are employed have to be interested in the labour process as it is about the details of what they are paid to do. So too, do managers need to be interested in the labour process. Braverman, in his critique of Taylorism, explains that behind it 'lies a theory which is nothing less than the explicit verbalization of the capitalist mode of production' (Braverman, 1998, 60). Taylor puts forwards an argument that speaks to the employers' unbridled interests in the employment relationship. Put in other terms, Taylorism involves three principles: first, the 'gathering and development of knowledge of the labour process;' second, 'the concentration of this knowledge as the exclusive province of management;' and third, the 'use of this monopoly over knowledge to control each step of the labor process and its mode of execution' (Braverman, 1998, 82).

The labour process has existed from the moment that an employment relationship was entered into. The labour process involves three parts: first, the 'purposeful activity, that is the work itself'; second, 'the subject of that work' and the materials being worked with; and third, 'the instruments involved', including tools, machinery, and so on (Marx, 1867, 284). For the analysis, this means metaphorically following the worker into what has been called the 'hidden abode of production' in which 'the secret of profit-making must at last be laid bare' (Marx, 1867, 280).

While for Taylor this was about identifying how profit-making could be maximised, with labour process theory this was about understanding the conflict inherent in the employment relationship. For both perspectives, this was about trying to understand the 'indeterminacy' of the labour process. As Richard Edwards has argued:

> Conflict exists because the interests of worker and those of employers collide … control is rendered problematic because unlike the other commodities involved in production, labor power is always embodied in people, who have their own interests and needs and who retain their power to resist being treated like a commodity.
>
> (Edwards, 1979, 12)

Labour process theory therefore tries to understand this conflict from the perspective of workers and the working process itself in the employment relationship. Importantly, it draws attention to this indeterminacy that is at the heart of many of the issues of employment that will be discussed throughout the book.

Braverman's *Labour and Monopoly Capital*, a critique of Taylorism, also represents another important theoretical development within the history of employment. Braverman makes an argument about the degradation of work that happens with increased attempts at management control. In particular, he focuses on the deskilling that takes place along with Taylorisation of work. Published in 1974, it also represents another attempt to understand employment as larger scale changes were unfolding. From the 1970s onwards, a range of important trends in employment pick up pace, including the growth of service work, changes in the global division of labour – and more that will be discussed in subsequent chapters. As Chris Smith has argued:

> *Labor and Monopoly Capital* cast a long shadow over debates on the nature of work in the late twentieth and early twenty first centuries. From the late 1970s a debate around the issue of the 'labour process' in capitalist society developed in many, but especially English-speaking, countries … The 'labour process' perspective on the ordering of work suggests that managerial action is chiefly motivated by capital-labour relations, by strategies of employers and their agents to try and control and stabilise the 'unruly' element/factor of production, namely living labour. The indeterminacy of labour is due to the fact that the employer buys a mere capacity to work when a worker is hired; an embodied capacity that walks into and out of the workplace, and must be managed with consent. Management must control or manage this capacity, and control is the raison d'être of management, the only reason it functions as a separate category of authority representing the global function of capital; otherwise it would just be another category or labour to be hired like other skilled workers.
>
> (Smith, 2009)

Similarly, Littler argued that 'Braverman's major contribution was to smash through the academic barriers and offer the potential for the birth of a new, integrated approach to the study and history of work' (Littler, 1982). However, there is relatively little about resistance and struggles over employment in the book.

Labour process theory often focuses on the issue of control in the workplace. This can involve trying to understand how effective management is carried out in practice. For example, through a 'system of control' that is part of 'the social relations of production within the firm'. There are three parts to this: first, 'direction' and the setting of out of how workers will complete tasks; second, 'evaluation' and the supervision and assessment of how workers are carrying out the tasks; and third, 'discipline' and the methods to 'elicit cooperation and enforce compliance with the capitalist's direction of the labour process' (Edwards, 1979, 18). However, the problem with employment is that 'complications arise when attempts are made to specify how control is acquired and maintained'. It can refer to both in 'an absolute sense, to identify those "in control"', and in a relative sense, to signify the degree of power people have to direct work' (Thompson,

1983, 123). Control has therefore also been conceptualised as a dynamics process, including with the 'frontier of control' in the workplace, subject to pressure from both workers and managers (Goodrich, 1975).

The main concepts that have been used in labour process theory are summarised by Chris Smith in Table 1.1 (Smith, 2005, 208–209).

STRUGGLES OVER EMPLOYMENT IN BRITAIN

Alongside the emergence of employment as a relationship there has always been tension and conflict between the two parties involved. Whether between artisans and Pharaohs, peasants and

Table 1.1 Main Concepts in Labour Process Analysis

1. **Labour Power** – a special commodity being part of the whole person of the worker and what is sold – a worker's labour time.

2. **Control imperative** – due to the absence of consensus on how much labour is extracted from workers through the labour process, the purchaser of labour power must seek the means to control this process – which can only ever be partially accomplished, as control is not absolute. The means of control can be through institutional norms of joint interests, technological controls, bureaucratic rules or self-management. Whatever the means, there is always a control imperative in the labour process.

3. The **labour process is one moment** in the cycle of commodity production. Before entering production labour power must be reproduced and hired; a commodity is produced and circulated and exchanged, before the money earned can re-enter the cycle of commodity production. Kelly (1985) looked at the labour process in relationship to product and money cycles.

4. **Technology/tools** – instruments of labour can be hand-held, powered or automated; technology is 'fixed capital'; it can be owned by the capitalist firm or society; and concentrated in special places – factories or offices for example – or distributed throughout society through 'mobile technologies' such as smart phones, tablets and computers.

5. **Purpose of production** – there is always a reason for bringing labour processes together, and these purposes are the drivers of production, whether for ends that are collective, public, or for private accumulation of wealth.

6. **Spatial divisions of labour**: largely absent from Marx and Braverman's discussion of the labour process was the spatial distribution of production and elements of the labour process – including workers. Increased geographical movement of labour and capital, can create what Harvey (2006) called a 'spatial fix', that capital can utilise in bargaining with governments and employees, that is movement or threat of closing workplaces in one country or locality can be used to bargain with states and workers' representatives, such threats often extracting concessions on working conditions and wages. Such threats are only possible because of the spread of the capitalist system geographically and the opening-up of new territories for expansion and re-location. At a macro level countries compete for Foreign Direct Investment and this can mobilise the distribution of 'human resources' by institutions like local authorities and schools to serve the demands of new entrants (see Smith and Chan, 2015). 'Space' is therefore an important element of management control and a factor of production – see also Harvey (2006), Massey (1984), Peck (1996) and McGrath-Champ, Herod and Rainnie (2010) who elaborate on the implications for the labour process of a more fluid understanding of space as resource for capital, and mobility as a resource for labour. All explore how labour markets develop alongside spatially embedded social and political institutions.

Table 1.1 (Cont.)

7. **Conflict** is at the centre of the relations between employers and workers as a structured interest antagonism, in other words something not contingent upon the subjective attitudes of either side. Marx forces us to consider the fundamental power imbalance between labour and capital – capital needs labour to expand; but labour needs capital to survive, and starvation and fear can be the whip that keeps waged labour at work. The collective power of labour, both structural and associative (Wright, 2000) is different for capital, which can move through different forms and store itself (in money) in different places (in housing property which is never used but held as exchange value in cities like London for example). As noted below labour power is embodied and cannot be transformed in the same way as capital which is an object, as well as subject. Although Marx, following Adam Smith, saw labour power as 'variable capital' (see below) it is important to note the substantive structural differences between both labour and capital. As a recent discussion by Hodgson (2014) notes, capital is money or a deposit external to the individual and in this sense '"human capital" can only be collateral if the humans involved are slaves. "Social capital" can never be used as collateral and it is not even owned.' This strict definition of capital does miss its' symbolic, emotional and status elements, which are part of the way it is represented beyond material form. But labour power cannot be stored or transformed – at least only in the short-run – while in moving within and outside one's country to work is always a possibility – controls on labour flows are greater than on capitals flows (Sassen, 1988) and migrant and illegal workers are always more vulnerable to super-exploitation (Anderson, 2010, 2013).

8. **Capitalism** – forms, trends, transitions and dynamics. Capitalism is historically the most dynamic production system, but it is difficult to plot a linear trend to the development of the labour process in capitalist societies. Edwards (1979) saw control cycles evolving through contradictions of conflicts between labour and capital, but more recently control has not been conceived in zero-sum or replacement terms, but as coexisting and multiple forms (Thompson and Hartley, 2007). As new countries are pulled into global capitalism, 'old forms' can be revised; or new technologies, allow renewal of old systems. Informalisation and the expansion of self-employment during the recession means decline in waged labour formally managed/controlled through the firm's bureaucratic hierarchy, and the rise of contractors, self-policing and control: '... developing economies are marked by the existence of an overwhelmingly large volume of economic activities that fall within what is described as the informal sector. It is an economic space in which workers engage in economic activities in ways that are very different from the capitalist organisation of production. In particular, the prevalent form of labour in the informal sector is self-employment, which is different from the usual wage-based employment resting on the alienation of labour from capital' (Sanyal and Bhattacharyya, 2009, 35). Informal working is now being researched more thoroughly in developed economies (Williams and Nadin, 2012).

9. **Labour process and labour markets**. Radical labour economists saw the labour market possessing divided, dual or segmented forms (Peck, 1996), and explored how different social categories of labour relate to these differentiated positions in the labour process and labour market (Gordon et al., 1982; Friedman, 1977). Writers continue to explore the connection between the labour market, social networks and labour process, examining the development of new informalities and old labour forms (Kalleberg, 2009), for example the return of gang labour in the UK (Strauss, 2013a) or the growth of third parties, such as employment agencies, in employment relationship (Enright, 2013; Strauss, 2013b).

Source: Table from Smith, 2005, 208–209

landlords, or workers and employers. The history of employment is filled with struggles over the what, how, when, who, and why of work. For example, the Peasant's Revolt in 1381 was a major uprising that spread across England, triggered by a poll tax. The peasants demanded an end to serfdom and to be paid (Oman, 1906, 200). Throughout the history that has followed there have been moments of resistance, hidden or open, that have been a key part of how employment has developed. Industrialisation brought factories and new concentrations of workers together, which laid the basis for new forms of workers' organisations. E.P. Thompson argues between 1790 and 1830 the formation of the working class began:

> By 1832 there were strongly based and self-conscious working-class institutions – trade unions, friendly societies, educational and religious movements, political organizations, periodicals – working class intellectual traditions, working-class community patterns and a working-class structure of feeling.
>
> (Thompson, 1991, 213)

In this moment the creation of new forms of work and employment was met with new social structures and forms of organisation. This history is not as simple as the factory or the industrial revolution creating unions, instead these processes interacted with the existing cultural traditions and ways of living, as well radical religious beliefs, to form something new. As E.P. Thompson continues, the 'making of the working class is a fact of political and cultural, as much as of economic history' (Thompson, 1991, 213). Class, in this sense, is a political category. However, work remains important for understanding class today (Toscano and Woodcock, 2015).

One of the most important institutions that has been established through these struggles over work and employment are trade unions. Trade unions – sometimes also called labour unions or just unions – are institutions that developed to advance or defend the collective interests of workers. They originated with forms of collective organising, negotiation, and bargaining between workers and employers, often taking place within a hostile environment.

While industrialisation was continuing at pace in England, the government at the time was against workers forming unions or any kind of collective organisation. The Combination Acts of 1799/1800 banned any sort of meeting that could lead to combined activities of workers to improve their conditions. Following the French Revolution, the Tory government was determined to stop workers' protests. With only a minority of men being able to vote, there were major campaigns to reform voting and extend franchise to workers. The Combination Acts were repealed in 1824 – although limitations were introduced a year later with the 1825 Combination Act – but unions developed rapidly. In particular, unions were established in the textile industry (Davis, 2004a).

By 1834 large, national organisations were developed. One example was the Grand National Consolidated Trades Union (GNCTU). However, this was opposed by the government. When six agricultural labourers met in Tolpuddle, Dorset to swear an oath to join, they were arrested. They became known as the Tolpuddle Martyrs and were sentenced to penal transportation to Australia. A mass campaign to defend them was launched, and while it was too late to stop their transportation to Australia, their sentenced were repealed and they were returned home (Davis, 2004a).

From 1834 to 1850, there were three mass campaigns of the new workers' movement. The first was Chartism, a political movement based on a six-point charter:

1. A vote for every man twenty-one years of age, of sound mind, and not undergoing punishment for crime.
2. The ballot – to protect the elector in the exercise of his vote.
3. No property qualification for Members of Parliament – thus enabling the constituencies to return the man of their choice, be he rich or poor.
4. Payment of members, thus enabling an honest tradesman, working man, or other person, to serve a constituency, when taken from his business to attend to the interests of the Country.
5. Equal constituencies, securing the same amount of representation for the same number of electors, instead of allowing small constituencies to swamp the votes of large ones.

6. Annual Parliaments, thus presenting the most effectual check to bribery and intimidation, since though a constituency might be bought once in seven years (even with the ballot), no purse could buy a constituency (under a system of universal suffrage) in each ensuing twelve-month; and since members, when elected for a year only, would not be able to defy and betray their constituents as now.

(Davis, 2004b)

Workers organised a General Strike in 1842, opposing both the 25% cut in wages that had been proposed by cotton factory owners, as well as demanding political rights. Alongside this, 'short time' committees were established that demanded the regulation of working hours and conditions in factories. Workers also mobilised against the Poor Law Amendment of 1834 which forced the poor into Workhouses. In 1848, revolutions swept across Europe, but in Britain the government was able to arrest the leaders of the Chartists and quell the movement (Davis, 2004b).

Following this, new industries were emerging in Britain, including iron, coal, and steel. From 1850, Britain was able to monopolise world trade, becoming the so-called 'workshop of the world'. The union movement also developed in a new direction during this period. Starting with the Amalgamated Society of Engineers in 1851 a new model of unionism emerged. These were national organisations that operated centrally, with members paying high dues to the union so it could hire officials. Negotiation with employers became more common, although there were large strikes during the period. Trade union membership grew rapidly during the period, from 100,000 in 1850 to over a million by 1874. While women had played an important role in early textile unions, they were increasingly excluded from the movement beyond that historic base. In 1868 the Trades Union Congress (TUC), which brought together different unions, was founded in Manchester (Davis, 2004c).

This was also a period in which legislation reshaped work and the employment relationship. The Reform Act 1867 extended voting to part of the urban male working class in England and Wales. After the Act, there were six key pieces of legislation introduced that changed regulation of work and trade unionism (Davis, 2004c).

Master and Servant Act 1867. Under the Act, striking workers could be prosecuted for breach of contract. This followed the Combination Act 1825 that had previously limited trade union rights only to bargaining over wages and conditions, anything more was criminalised. The Act reserved the right for criminal action in certain cases.

Trade Union Act 1871. This Act legalised trade unions for the first time. They were recognised as legal entities that had full protection of their funds. The 'restraint of trade' doctrine, which had been used in previous regulation to limit unions and combinations, would no longer apply.

Criminal Law Amendment Act 1871. Passed on the same day at the Trade Union Act 1871, it made picketing (protesting outside of a workplace during a strike, often to persuade others to take part) illegal.

Factories (Health of Women, &c.) Act 1874. Introduce a ten-hour day working limit. Trade unions had been campaigning for an eight-hour day, but this was an improvement for many workers.

Conspiracy and Protection of Property Act 1875. This decriminalised many aspects of trade union activity, including picketing. Trade unions could not be prosecuted for acts that would be legal for an individual. Trade union disputes therefore became civil, rather than criminal, matters.

Employers and Workmen Act 1875. This introduced breaches of contracts for both 'employers' and 'workmen' in civil law. Previously, employers could be liable for a fine, while those employed could be subject to criminal law, fines, and imprisonment.

From the 1880s, a mass labour movement was established in Britain (Webb and Webb, 1975). Trade unions were established in new industries, including the gasworks and the docks (Tillett, 1910), while women workers at the Bryant and May factory organised a successful and high-profile strike (Raw, 2009). This was a period of 'new unionism' in which workers campaigned for an eight-hour day. However, by the late 1800s, there were further attempts by employers to limit the powers of trade unions, including legal cases once again trying to criminalise strikes and picketing. By 1914, over 90% of trade union members were men and the overwhelming majority of women workers were not part of the trade union movement. However, women organised outside of the existing trade union movement, including the Women's Trade Union League, the Co-operative Women's Guild, and the National Federation of Women Workers. Women workers organised around the fight for the vote and there was substantial crossover with the labour movement. For example, the Women's Social and Political Union (WSPU), formed by Emmeline, Sylvia, and Christabel Pankhurst, had strong connections to the labour movement (Rowbotham, 1977). While the rest of the movement was slow to support women's suffrage, there were also important splits, like Sylvia Pankhurst's focus on organising with working-class women in East London and the labour movement, which led to her expulsion from the WSPU (Davis, 2004d).

The First World War had a substantial effect on employment, as well as struggles against it. Millions of young men in Britain, as well as across Europe and the world, were drawn into military service and killed. While there was opposition in the run-up to the war, both the Labour party and the TUC declared an 'industrial truce' and supported recruitment for the war (Davis, 2004e). Following the First World War, there was a widespread wave of strikes in 1919. This took place against a backdrop of worker uprisings in Germany and Hungary, as well as revolution in Russia (Davis, 2004f). In 1926, there was a general strike (a strike that takes place across multiple sectors, often involving workers taking solidarity action). Workers across Britain took strike action in support of miners. They strike lasted nine days, but was called off by the TUC, ending in defeat (Laybourn, 1993). The Conservative government took advantage of the defeat to bring in further anti-trade union legislation, including The Trade Disputes and Trade Union Act 1927 which limited strikes to the trade or industry involved and outlawed sympathy or solidarity strikes.

The union movement was weakened for the following decade. This was followed by the Second World War, in which a similar curtailing of the movement took place again in response. Legislation was introduced that banned strikes, although they would continue to take place. An important shift during the war was that many more women entered the workforce. Following 1941, women were conscripted either in industries like munitions or into agriculture in the Land Army. This led to debates about the introduction of state-run nurseries. However, the settlement for the burden of childcare was pushed back on to women. As Mary Davis argues:

> the more convenient and ideologically acceptable expedient of adjusting women to their double burden by permitting them to work part-time was the favoured alternative. Such a 'concession' was one of the few wartime changes which remains as a permanent feature of women's labour and of course helps to account for continuing low wages and lack of job opportunity.
>
> (Davis, 2004g)

After the Second World War, a Labour party majority was elected in 1945. Facing pressure from a working class that had only just been demobilised from fighting in a war, the government embarked on a programme of nationalisation and the building of a welfare state. This involved the introduction of a national insurance programme for sickness and unemployment, covering workplace injuries, and the establishment of the National Health Service (Davis, 2004h). These policies were a huge victory for workers (Wahl, 2011). In the 1950s, trade unions became an important part of how employment was organised, particularly in manufacturing. This also saw the entry of more younger workers into unions, including those starting campaigns to unionise white-collar work. Towards the end of the 1950s, there were successful national strikes in shipbuilding and engineering. This was a high point of struggle not seen since 1926 (Fishman, 2004a).

The 1960s were a period of broader social change within which workers and unions played an important role. This was a decade of national liberation struggles, strikes, student protests, and new forms of counterculture. People across the world took part in social movements that included many social issues, but also the organisation of employment (Mohandesi et al., 2018). In France, this came close to revolution with workers on strike and students occupying their universities (Abidor, 2018). In Britain, unions 'responded with sincere, and often successful, initiatives to adapt the culture of trade unionism to take account of the changes', including trying to extend their 'reach towards the second wave of feminism and youth culture. There were also determined attempts to address issues of racism at the workplace and inside trade unions' (Fishman, 2004b). Trade union density reached 55.4% in 1979, with 13 million members in Britain. The union movement expanded into new sectors, including office and technical work. Throughout the 1960s the government responded. It is a period that was 'remarkable for the extent to which successive governments became involved in legislating and regulating terms and conditions of employment' (Fishman, 2004b). A range of new legislation covered minimum periods of notice for sacking workers, redundancy protections, and the necessity of contract details. Following strikes of women workers at the Ford Dagenham plant and other struggles, the Equal Pay Act 1970 was introduced that required employers to pay men and women doing the same work an equal wage.

By the 1970s, trade union struggles had reached a peak. There were strikes of miners and dockers in the early 1970s. This included a national dock strike in which five dockworkers were arrested and imprisoned, then freed under the pressure of the strikers. The national disputes were so intense that by 1974 they led to an emergency general election with the slogan 'Who governs Britain?'. This was an attempt to pitch the election as between the Conservatives and the National Union of Mineworkers (NUM), rather than against the Labour party (Fishman, 2004c). This was period of militancy from the rank-and-file membership of trade unions, sometimes called shop stewards. Similar dynamics were also taking place in the USA (Brenner et al., 2010). As Nina Fishman notes, this was not only about large strikes: 'An additional cause for concern was the increasing number of unofficial strikes in engineering in the 1970s. Some factories seemed to be particularly strike-prone. Workers went on strike, it seemed, not to gain significant concessions, but for a small point of principle' (Fishman, 2004d).

The 1980s is often seen as a turning point for the trade union movement, changing struggles against employment. As Dave Lyddon argued:

> In the 1980s and 1990s, the British trade union movement faced several inter-related challenges: high levels of unemployment and the continuing contraction of many well unionised industries; privatisation of most nationalised industries and the increasing use of private contractors in many public services; a Conservative government openly hostile to trade unions and legislating against them; and, feeding off these, a more aggressive attitude from both private and public sector employers and managers to unions and shop stewards defending the terms and conditions of their members.
>
> (Lyddon, 2004)

These changes in employment at the sectoral or economy-wide level changed the terrain on which workers and unions were organising. There were large strikes of NHS workers, teachers, and local government workers. However, the most defining dispute of the period is the miners' strike of 1984–1985. This dispute became a national struggle between the NUM and the government over the closure of coal pits. Over the two years, the government deployed a huge number of police, arresting over 11,000 people. There was a widespread network of support for the miners, but it was not met with sympathy strikes – which had been made unlawful – or the kind of union solidarity that had made the disputes in the early 1970s so effective (Lyddon, 2004). The defeat of the miners' strike, like that of the air traffic controllers in the USA, became a key turning point in the union movement. From that point onwards, union membership and power has steadily declined. The reasons and implications of this will be considered in subsequent chapters.

This period also saw significant changes in legislation of employment:

The Employment Act 1982. Introduced restrictions on industrial action, particularly limiting strikes to those targeted the employer. It also undermined union 'closed shop' arrangements.

Trade Union Act 1984. Introduced requirements of secret ballots for union executive officials and industrial action.

Employment Act 1990. Made all secondary strike action unlawful. It also became unlawful to refuse employment to non-union members, further undermining union closed shops.

Trade Union and Labour Relations (Consolidation) Act 1992. This defined trade unions and their duties. It covered both protections for workers in unions, as well as those who wanted to leave them.

Trade Union Reform and Employment Rights Act 1993. This brought in major changes to the operation of unions, including the requirement for all industrial action ballots to be carried out by post.

The Employment Tribunals Act 1996. This established a system of Employment Tribunals that could make judgements on issues arising out of employment contracts and other Acts.

These changed the relationships between workers and employers, as well as between workers and unions, and unions and employers. The dynamics between these different interests and actors has greatly shaped the kinds of employment relations that are present today. It is worth noting that there is an important distinction to make here. Workers have their own interests – whether that be in their own workplaces, across industries and sectors, or so on. Often, these interests can be aligned with the unions they are members of. However, there are also points in which the interests of unions have diverged from workers' interests. This can be seen with the rise of rank-and-file organising in the 1970s, or increasingly since the defeats of the miners' strike. Unions cannot be only taken as a proxy for workers interests.

At the core, trade unions can be defined by what Blackburn called their 'unionateness', that is the

> collective bargaining and the protection of the interests of members, as employees, as its main function, rather than, say, professional activities or welfare schemes … It is independent of employers for purposes of negotiation … It is prepared to be militant, using all forms of industrial action which may be effective.
>
> (Blackburn, 1967, 19)

While this may cover similar interests to workers, it is also worth noting that some unions have diverged in practice from this model. In some cases, this involves working in partnership with employers, or focusing more on service provision.

Despite these complications, it is clear that the trade union movement has had a significant impact on the employment relationship. Taking Britain as an example, it has been pivotal in the following:

1. Introducing the 9 to 5 working day
2. Increasing the amount of annual leave
3. Forcing employers to abide by contracts
4. Lifting restrictions on parental leave
5. Tackling discrimination at work
6. Helping to introduce the minimum wage
7. Providing a way for workers to talk to management about pay and conditions
8. Proved the power of the petition
9. The weekend as a rest break

The history also shows an important point: that employment is a dynamic phenomenon.

THE EMPLOYMENT RELATIONSHIP TODAY

This history of work is important for shaping the ways in which employment is organised today. What has hopefully been clear throughout this chapter is that employment and work has never taken just a single form. There are a wide variety of ways that work has been organised and the employment relationship has also taken many forms. Employment has been a changing phenomenon since the beginning. It has evolved as the different interests involved have fought for changes in different directions.

Despite these changes, the literature often talks about the 'standard employment relationship'. Or rather, this standard employment relationship is sometimes discussed as what is being transformed with new changes, whether through the emergence of different kinds of work, technology, or relationships. The standard employment relationship refers to a very specific time and place. In particular, it is often used to describe the kinds of working relationships found in the Global North after the Second World War. This already limits it significantly both in terms of a timeframe and location, let alone the people who experienced it. For workers, this employment relationship involved the expectation of a 'stable, socially protected, dependent, full-time job ... the basic conditions of which (working time, pay, social transfers) are regulated to a minimum level by collective agreement or by labour and/or social security law' (Bosch, 2004, 618).

This standard employment relationship is not only about the employment relationship between worker and employer, but also about the relationship between this and the 'wider risk-sharing role of the welfare or social state', which came to prominence in parts of the Global North by the mid-20th century (Fudge, 2017, 379). This is an important context that provided many of the additional benefits. For example, the risk of employment could be mitigated both with agreements in the workplace, but also social security, healthcare, available housing, and so on beyond that. The risk with using this term is that it implies something about this having been a standard for many people. However, for the majority of people in employment — let alone those aside of it — the 'relative stability and security of employment in the West post-WWII ... was an anomaly' (Bent, 2017, 3). This stability was also often only available to white men in the Global North, often excluding women and minorities. Indeed, while there has been a resurgence of research interest in precarious work (that is unstable relationships, which will be discussed later in the book), it is 'not necessarily new or novel to the current era; it has existed since the launch of paid employment as a primary source of sustenance' (Kalleberg, 2009, 2).

Table 1.2 Employment Relations in Contemporary Britain

An employer must provide employees with:	Employers must also:
a written statement of employment or contract	make sure employees do not work longer than the maximum allowed
the statutory minimum level of paid holiday	pay employees at least the minimum wage
a payslip showing all deductions, such as National Insurance contributions (NICs)	have employer's liability insurance
the statutory minimum length of rest breaks	provide a safe and secure working environment
Statutory Sick Pay (SSP)	register with HM Revenue and Customs to deal with payroll, tax, and NICs
maternity, paternity, and adoption pay and leave	consider flexible working requests
	avoid discrimination in the workplace
	make reasonable adjustments to your business premises if your employee is disabled

Source: Adapted from gov.uk, 2022

The standard employment relationship might therefore be seen a sort of high point of employment protections and benefits, albeit one also tied to the social relations of the specific context. The risk with seeing the employment relationship as stable is that it misses much of the diversity in relationships that takes place under the category of employment. What the critical history of employment shows is that there are a wide variety of different ways in which both work and employment can be organised. What is common across all of these relationships is that the labour process brings together labour-power with management. These relationships of work are determined in practice by the relative power of workers (selling their time) and capital (buying that time) within the social contexts in which work is carried out. It should therefore not be a surprise to see many different kinds of practices within employment, both now and over time and space.

Today, employment is covered by state regulation and laws. For example, in the UK there are the following requirements for employment:

However, in other jurisdictions and contexts, these kinds of rights can be very different. For example, in 74% of countries across the world workers do not have the right to establish or join a trade union. Approximately 60% of people work in informal employment, with no rights or protections (ITUC, 2022). The best rating in the Global Rights Index carried out by the International Trade Union Confederation is 'sporadic violation of rights', which only includes Austria, Denmark, Finland, Germany, Iceland, Ireland, Italy, Norway, and Sweden. Britain falls into rating 3 'regular violation of rights', while the USA falls in rating 4 'systematic violation of rights' (ITUC, 2022). This means there is huge variation in how employment is experienced by workers in practice.

REFERENCES

Abidor, M. (2018) *May made me: an oral history of the 1968 uprising in France*, London, Pluto Press.

Anderson, B. (2010) 'Migration, Immigration Controls and the Fashioning of Precarious Workers', *Work, Employment and Society*, vol. 24, no. 2, pp. 300–317.

Anderson, B. (2013) *Us and Them?: the Dangerous Politics of Immigration Control*, Oxford, Oxford University Press.

Anderson, P. (1974) *Passages from Antiquity to Feudalism*, London, Verso.

Arendt, H. (1998) *The human condition*, 2nd edn, Chicago, University of Chicago Press.

Banaji, J. (2020) *A brief history of commercial capitalism*, Chicago, Illinois, Haymarket Books.

Bent, P. (2017) 'Historical Perspectives on Precarious Work: The Cases of Egypt and India under British Imperialism', *Global Labour Journal*, vol. 8, no. 1, pp. 3–16.

Blackburn, R. (1967) *Union Character and Social Class*, London, Batsford.

Blackburn, R. (2010) *The making of New World slavery: from the Baroque to the Modern, 1492–1800*, London; New York, Verso.

Bosch, G. (2004) 'Towards a New Standard Employment Relationship in Western Europe', *British Journal of Industrial Relations*, vol. 42, no. 4, pp. 617–636.

Braverman, H. (1998) *Labor and Monopoly Capital: The Degradation of Work in the Twentieth Century*, New York, Monthly Review Press.

Brenner, A., Brenner, R. and Winslow, C. (eds) (2010) *Rebel rank and file: labor militancy and revolt from below during the long 1970s*, London; New York, Verso.

Brenner, R. (1976) 'Agrarian class structure and economic development in pre-industrial Europe', *Past and Present*, vol. 70, no. 170, pp. 30–75.

Brenner, R. (1977) 'The origins of capitalist development: a critique of neo-Smithian Marxism', *New Left Review*, vol. 104, pp. 121–140.

Davis, M. (2004a) *1815–1834* [Online]. Available at http://unionhistory.info/timeline/1815_1834.php.

Davis, M. (2004b) *1834–1850* [Online]. Available at http://unionhistory.info/timeline/1834_1850.php.

Davis, M. (2004c) *1850–1880* [Online]. Available at http://unionhistory.info/timeline/1850_1880.php.

Davis, M. (2004d) *1880–1914* [Online]. Available at http://unionhistory.info/timeline/1880_1914.php.

Davis, M. (2004e) *1914–1918* [Online]. Available at http://unionhistory.info/timeline/1914_1918.php.

Davis, M. (2004f) *1918–1939* [Online]. Available at http://unionhistory.info/timeline/1918_1939.php.

Davis, M. (2004g) *1939–1945* [Online]. Available at http://unionhistory.info/timeline/1939_1945.php.

Davis, M. (2004h) *1945–1960* [Online]. Available at http://unionhistory.info/timeline/1945_1960.php.

Dobb, M. (1946) *Studies in the Development of Capitalism*, New York, International Publishers.

Edgerton, W.F. (1951) 'The Strikes in Ramses III's Twenty-Ninth Year', *Journal of Near Eastern Studies*, vol. 10, no. 3, pp. 137–415.

Edwards, R. (1979) *Contested terrain: The transformation of the workplace in the twentieth century*, New York, Basic Books.

Eltis, D. and Richardson, D. (2015) *Atlas of the transatlantic slave trade*, New Haven, CT, Yale University Press.

Engels, F. (1844) *The Condition of the Working Class in England*, 2009, Oxford, Oxford University Press.

Enright, B. (2013) '(Re) considering new agents: a review of labour market intermediaries within labour geography', *Geography Compass*, vol. 7, no. 4, pp. 287–299.

Fishman, N. (2004a) *1951–1960* [Online]. Available at http://unionhistory.info/timeline/1945_1960_2.php.

Fishman, N. (2004b) *1960–2000 Part 1* [Online]. Available at http://unionhistory.info/timeline/1960_2000.php.

Fishman, N. (2004c) *1960–2000 Part 3* [Online]. Available at http://unionhistory.info/timeline/1960_2000_3.php.

Fishman, N. (2004d) *1960–2000 Part 4* [Online]. Available at http://unionhistory.info/timeline/1960_2000_4.php.

Friedman, A.F. (1977) *Industry and Labour*, London, Macmillan.

Fudge, J. (2017) 'The Future of the Standard Employment Relationship: Labour Law, New Institutional Economics and Old Power Resource Theory', *Journal of Industrial Relations*, vol. 59, no. 3, pp. 374–392.

Genovese, E.D. (1988) *The World the Slaveholders Made*, Middletown, CT, Wesleyan University Press.

Goodrich, C.L. (1975) *The Frontier of Control: A Study in British Workshop Politics*, London, Pluto Press.

Gordon, D.M., Edwards, R. and Reich, M. (1982) *Segmented Work, Divided Workers: The Historical Transformation of Labor in the United States*, Cambridge, Cambridge University Press.

gov.uk (2022) *Contract types and employer responsibilities* [Online]. Available at www.gov.uk/contract-types-and-employer-responsibilities/fulltime-and-parttime-contracts.

Graeber, D. and Wengrow, D. (2021) *The dawn of everything: a new history of humanity*, London, Allen Lane.

Harman, C. (2004) 'The Rise of Capitalism', *International Socialism*, vol. 102.

Harvey, D. (2006) *The Limits to Capital*, London, Verso.

Heller, H. (2011) *The birth of capitalism: a twenty-first-century perspective*, The future of world capitalism, London, Pluto Press.

Hobbes, T. (2008) *Leviathan*, Gaskin, J.C.A. (ed), Oxford world's classics, Oxford, Oxford University Press.

Hodgskin, T. (1832) *The Natural and Artificial Right of Property Contrasted*, London, B. Steil.

Hodgson, G.M. (2014) 'What is capital? Economists and sociologists have changed its meaning: should it be changed back?', *Cambridge Journal of Economics*, vol. 38, no. 5, pp. 1063–1086 [Online]. DOI: 10.1093/cje/beu013.

ITUC (2022) *2022 ITUC Global Rights Index*, Brussels, International Trade Union Confederation.

Kalleberg, A.L. (2009) 'Precarious Work, Insecure Workers: Employment Relations in Transition', *American Sociological Review*, vol. 74, no. 1, pp. 1–22.

Kelly, J. (1985) 'Cycles of Control', in Knights, D., Willmott, H. and Collinson, D. (eds), *Job Redesign: Critical Perspectives on the Labour Process*, London, Gower.

Laybourn, K. (1993) *The General Strike of 1926*, New frontiers in history, Manchester, Manchester University Press.

Littler, C.R. (1982) *The Development of the Labour Process in Capitalist Societies: A Comparative Study of the Transformation of Work Organization in Britain, Japan and the USA*, London, Heinemann Educational Books.

Lyddon, D. (2004) *1960–2000 Part 7* [Online]. Available at http://unionhistory.info/timeline/1960_2000_7.php.

Marx, K. (1867) *Capital: A Critique of Political Economy Vol. 1*, 1976, London, Penguin Books.

Marx, K. (1973) *Grundrisse: foundations of the critique of political economy*, Harmondsworth, Penguin Books.

Marx, K. and Engels, F. (1848) *The Communist Manifesto*, [Online]. Available at www.marxists.org/archive/marx/works/1848/communist-manifesto/ch01.htm#007.

Marx, K. and Engels, F. (1932) 'The German ideology'.

Massey, D. (1984) *The Spatial Divisions of Labour*, New York, Routledge.

McGrath-Champ, S., Herod, A. and Rainnie, A. (eds) (2010) *Handbook of Employment and Society: Working Space*, Cheltenham, Edward Elgar Publishing.

Mintz, S.W. (1985) *Sweetness and power: the place of sugar in modern history*, New York, N.Y., Viking.

Mohandesi, S., Risager, B.S. and Cox, L. (2018) *Voices of 1968: documents from the global North*, London, Pluto Press.

Montgomery, D. (1987) *The fall of the house of labor: the workplace, the state, and American labor activism, 1865–1925*, Cambridge, Cambridge University Press.

Oman, C. (1906) *The Great Revolt of 1381*, Oxford, Clarendon Press.

Peck, J. (1996) *Work-place: The Social Regulation of Labor Markets*, New York, The Guilford Press.

Raw, L. (2009) *Striking A Light: The Bryant and May Matchwomen and their Place in History*, London, Continuum Books.

Robinson, J. (1962) *Economic Philosophy*, Chicago, Aldine Publishing.

Rowbotham, S. (1977) *Hidden from history: 300 years of women's oppression and the fight against it*, London, Pluto Press.

Sahlins, M. (2004) 'The Original Affluent Society', in Delaney, C.L. (ed), *Investigating culture: an experiential introduction to anthropology*, Oxford, Blackwell, pp. 110–133.

Sample, R.J. (2003) 'Exploitation: What It Is and Why It's Wrong', Rowman & Littlefield, Oxford.

Sanyal, K. and Bhattacharyya, R. (2009) 'Beyond the factory: globalisation, Informalisation of production and the new locations of labour', *Economic and Political Weekly*, pp. 35–44.

Sassen, S. (1988) *The Mobility of Labor and Capital*, Cambridge, Cambridge University Press.

Smith, A. (1999a) *The Wealth of Nations: Books I-III*, London, Penguin.

Smith, A. (1999b) *The Wealth of Nations: Books IV-V*, London, Penguin.

Smith, C. (2005) 'Rediscovery of the Labour Process', in Edgell, S., Gottfried, H. and Granter, E. (eds), *The SAGE Handbook of the Sociology of Work and Employment*, London, SAGE, pp. 205–224.

Smith, C. (2009) *The short overview of the labour process perspective and history of the International Labour Process Conference* [Online]. Available at www.ilpc.org.uk.

Smith, C. and Chan, J. (2015) 'Working for Two Bosses: Student Interns as Constrained Labour in China', *Human Relations*, vol. 68, no. 2, pp. 305–326.

Stanley, A.D. (1998) *From bondage to contract: wage labor, marriage, and the market in the age of slave emancipation*, Cambridge, Cambridge University Press.

Strauss, K. (2013a) 'Unfree again: social reproduction, flexible labour markets and the resurgence of gang labour in the UK', *Antipode*, vol. 45, no. 1, pp. 180–197.

Strauss, K. (2013b) 'Unfree Labour and the Regulation of Temporary Agency Work in the UK', in Fudge, J. and Strauss, K. (eds), *Temporary Work, Agencies, and Unfree Labor: Insecurity in the New World of Work*, London, Routledge.

Tawney, R.H. (1926) *Religion and the Rise of Capitalism: A Historical Study*, London, J. Murray.

Taylor, F.W. (1967) *The Principles of Scientific Management*, New York, Norton.

Thompson, E.P. (1967) 'Time, work-discipline and industrial capitalism', *Past and Present*, vol. 38, no. 1, pp. 56–97.

Thompson, E.P. (1991) *The Making of the English Working Class*, London, Penguin.

Thompson, P. (1983) *The nature of work: an introduction to debates on the labour process*, London, Macmillan [Online]. Available at http://books.google.com/books?id=qwzGAAAAIAAJ (Accessed 28 February 2022).

Thompson, P. and Hartley, B. (2007) 'HRM and the worker: Labor process perspectives', in *The Oxford Handbook of Human Resource Management*, Oxford, Oxford University Press.

Tillett, B. (1910) *A Brief History of the Dockers' Union*, London, Dock.

Toscano, A. and Woodcock, J. (2015) 'Spectres of Marxism: A Comment on Mike Savage's market model of class difference', *The Sociological Review*, vol. 63, pp. 512–523.

UK Parliament (2022) *The 1833 Factory Act* [Online]. Available at www.parliament.uk/about/living-heritage/transformingsociety/livinglearning/19thcentury/overview/factoryact/.

Wahl, A. (2011) *The Rise and Fall of the Welfare State*, London, Pluto Press.

Wallerstein, I. (1974) *The Modern World-System, Vol. 1: Capitalist Agriculture and the Origins of the European World-Economy*, New York, Academic Press.

Webb, S. and Webb, B. (1975) *The History of Trade Unionism*, New York, AMS Press.

Weber, M. (1930) *The Protestant Ethic and the Spirit of Capitalism*, London, Unwin Hyman.

Williams, C.C. and Nadin, S. (2012) 'Work beyond Employment', *Work, Employment and Society*, vol. 26, pp. 1–10.

Williams, E. (1994) *Capitalism and Slavery*, London, The University of North Carolina Press.

Woodcock, J. (2020) 'Exploitation', in Ritzer, G. and Rojek, C. (eds), *The Blackwell Encyclopedia of Sociology*, Oxford, John Wiley & Sons.

Wright, E. O. (2000) 'Working-Class Power, Capitalist-Class Interests and Class Compromise', *The American Journal of Sociology*, vol. 105, no. 4, pp. 957–1002.

CHAPTER 2

THE GLOBAL DIVISION OF LABOUR

A chapter on the global division of labour is a significant undertaking. Rather than try to explain how the division of labour is expressed across each country and every sector, this chapter instead will provide a global overview on dynamics of employment as shaped by these broad divisions. One of the challenges of thinking about the global division of labour is one of statistics. Employment is constantly changing and shifting. By the time you could build an accurate picture of employment (even at a local level, let alone global) the realities would have changed underneath. However, the fact is that one country – and in this case due to where the author lives, Britain – becomes used as though it is an exemplar of employment, or indeed that employment everywhere else must be broadly similar.

This chapter starts by tracing out employment across the world, examining higher level statistics. The next part introduces imperialism as a key driver of these changes, both historically and today. The chapter then moves on to discuss some key changes that are reshaping global employment, particularly discussing how work or workers can move. Unemployment is considered next, as well as the different kinds of informal work that many people are engaged in. Finally, the chapter considers alternatives to employment.

EMPLOYMENT ACROSS THE WORLD

Historically, collecting data on employment has relied on a variety of different measures, including surveys, self-reporting from employers, government agencies, other investigations, and often tax records. There are problems with all of these measures, often resulting in undercounting in key areas. However, there are broad outlines of employment that can be used to make some comparisons. In Table 2.1, employment status by region in 2021 is presented.

There are, of course, problems with grouping countries into regions (let alone grouping regions and areas into countries), but it gives a broad impression of the overall differences in employment across the world. For this analysis, the following categories are used. The first four cover those in employment: 'employees', 'own-account workers', 'contributing family workers', and 'employers' (adding up to a total of 100%). A further category of unemployment, 'unemployed', is added – although this will be discussed in more detail later in the chapter.

As can be seen from the definitions in Table 2.2, 'employees' is the formal category of employment, with a clear worker-employer relationship. The 'own-account workers' category is less formal, covering forms of what could be considered bogus self-employment (which will be discussed in later chapters). 'Contributing family workers' is a category tied to a particular way of organising employment with family relationships, for example a shop or other family business. Finally, 'employers' blurs the boundaries as they are also employing others in their business.

As can be seen from Table 2.1, there are substantial differences in the kinds of employment that are common. The global average has 53.4% of employment as employees, but substantial numbers of own-account workers (33.3%) and contributing family workers (10.2), with a smaller number of employers (3.1%). In addition to this, there is, on average, a 6.2% rate of unemployment. However, there is significant variation between regions. For example, rates of employees are highest in Northern America (92.5%) and lowest in sub-Saharan Africa (22.8%); own-account workers are highest in Southern Asia (53.7%) and lowest in Northern America

DOI: 10.4324/9781003279907-3

Table 2.1 Employment Status by Region 2021

	Employees	Own-account workers	Contributing family workers	Employers	Unemployed
Global	53.4%	33.3%	10.2%	3.1%	6.2%
Northern Africa	64.9%	21.9%	7.2%	6%	12.9%
Sub-Saharan Africa	22.8%	54.3%	20.7%	2.2%	7.3%
Latin America and the Caribbean	61.2%	30.1%	4.7%	4%	10%
Northern America	92.5%	4.9%	0.1%	2.5%	5.7%
Arab States	81.6%	12.9%	2.3%	3.2%	9.6%
Central and Western Asia	67.6%	20.7%	8.2%	3.5%	9.8%
Eastern Asia	58.4%	28.2%	9.6%	3.8%	4.6%
South-Eastern Asia and the Pacific	51.4%	33.2%	12.5%	2.8%	3.2%
Southern Asia	29.4%	53.7%	14.4%	2.5%	6%
Eastern Europe	89.2%	8.3%	0.7%	1.8%	5.3%
Northern, Southern and Western Europe	85.8%	9.4%	0.8%	4%	7.3%

Source: Adapted from ILO, 2022

(4.9%); contributing family workers are highest in sub-Saharan Africa (20.7%) and lowest in Northern America (0.1%); employers are highest in Northern Africa (6%) and lowest in Eastern Europe (1.8%); and unemployment rates vary from a high point in Northern Africa (12.9%) to the lowest in South-Eastern Asia and the Pacific (3.25). In some cases, the differences are almost 70%. In nine regions out of eleven, employee is the most common category.

Although there are some trends that emerge from looking over the differences by region, these become clearer when arranging employment status by income groups of countries. The ILO uses the World Bank Country and Lending Groups categories:

- Low-income economies are defined as those with a GNI per capita, calculated using the World Bank Atlas method, of $1,085 or less in 2021
- Lower middle-income economies are those with a GNI per capita between $1,086 and $4,255
- Upper middle-income economies are those with a GNI per capita between $4,256 and $13,205
- High-income economies are those with a GNI per capita of $13,205 or more

(The World Bank, 2022)

Dividing countries into these four groups provides a way to see a relationship between global inequality and employment status. Table 2.3 'Employment Status by Income Groups 2021' shows these differences.

There is a proportional increase in the rates of employees in employment across low-income to high-income countries. This is matched by reductions in the numbers of both own-account workers and contributing family workers from high-income to low-income countries. It is not the case that employment status is the reason that some countries are low-income while others are high-income. Table 2.4 'Employment Sector by Income Groups 2020' highlights what kinds of work people are doing, which can also help to explain these differences:

Table 2.2 Employment Status Definitions

Employment	Employees	'Employees are all those workers who hold paid employment jobs, which are those where the incumbents hold employment contracts which give them a basic remuneration not directly dependent upon the revenue of the unit for which they work.'
	Own-account workers	'Own-account workers are those workers who, working on their own account or with one or more partners, hold the type of jobs defined as a "self-employment jobs", and have not engaged on a continuous basis any employees to work for them.'
	Contributing family workers	'Contributing family workers are those workers who hold "self- employment jobs" as own-account workers in a market- oriented establishment operated by a related person living in the same household.'
	Employers	'Employers are those workers who, working on their own account or with one or a few partners, hold the type of jobs defined as a "self- employment jobs" (i.e. jobs where the remuneration is directly dependent upon the profits derived from the goods and services produced), and, in this capacity, have engaged, on a continuous basis, one or more persons to work for them as employee(s).'
Unemployment	Unemployed	'Persons in unemployment are defined as all those of working age who were not in employment, carried out activities to seek employment during a specified recent period AND were currently available to take up employment given a job opportunity.'

Source: Adapted from ILO, 2022

Table 2.3 Employment Status by Income Groups 2021

	Employees	Own-account workers	Contributing family workers	Employers	Unemployed
Low-income countries	18.9%	54.2%	24.9%	2%	5.9%
Lower-middle income countries	36.3%	47.2%	13.8%	2.7%	5.9%
Upper-middle income countries	60.6%	27.6%	8.1%	3.8%	6.7%
High-income countries	87.9%	7.9%	0.8%	3.3%	5.6%

Source: Adapted from ILO, 2022

What is clear when looking at employment sector by income groups of countries is that there are stark differences between the sectors of work. Low and lower-middle income countries have much larger levels of employment in agriculture, while upper-middle and high-income countries have much larger levels of employment in services. The kinds of work that people are doing therefore has a relationship to income levels.

Table 2.4 Employment Sector by Income Groups 2020

	Services	*Industry*	*Agriculture*
Low-income countries	10%	30.5%	59.4%
Lower-middle income countries	38.6%	20.3%	41.1%
Upper-middle income countries	53.7%	24.5%	21.7%
High-income countries	74.2%	22.7%	3%

Source: Adapted from ILO, 2022

IMPERIALISM

Considering these facts in the abstract of world history could give the impression that development is simply a question of employing more people to work in services. However, this would make little sense in practice. Societies rely on a combination of services, industries, and agriculture in order to survive and no country is self-sustaining, instead relying on international trade. Therefore, to understand how this current global division of labour emerged, it is necessary to place these current statistics within a historical context. A key factor in understanding this history is imperialism. This has been touched on in the previous chapter with the discussion of the transatlantic slave trade and the role this played in the development of capitalism. However, these processes of exploitation did not start and finish with slavery. Given how widely the term is often used, it is important to stress that imperialism has an economic foundation:

1. the concentration of production and capital has developed to such a high stage that it has created monopolies which play a decisive role in economic life;
2. the merging of bank capital with industrial capital, and the creation, on the basis of this 'finance capital,' of a financial oligarchy;
3. the export of capital as distinguished from the export of commodities acquires exceptional importance;
4. the formation of international monopolist capitalist associations which share the world among themselves and
5. the territorial division of the whole world among the biggest capitalist powers is completed.

(Lenin, 1965, 106)

Taken together:

> Imperialism is capitalism at that stage of development at which the dominance of monopolies and finance capital is established; in which the export of capital has acquired pronounced importance; in which the division of the world among the international trusts has begun, in which the division of all territories of the globe among the biggest capitalist powers has been completed.
>
> (Lenin, 1965, 106)

In practice, this means the reorganisation – often enforced with violence – of relationships across the world.

There are also forms of colonialism that have deeply shaped these global relationships. As Sai Englert argues, 'franchise colonial regimes rule the colonised through a mixture of military power, colonial administrators and collaborating local ruling classes', for example British colonial rule in India (Englert, 2022, 5). Settler colonialist formations '(aim to) make colonised lands their permanent home and in the process enter into continuous and sustained conflict with the Indigenous populations, whom they (attempt to) dispossess, exploit and/or eliminate', for example with European colonies in Argentina, Algeria, and Australia (Englert, 2022, 5–6).

In terms of what this means for employment today, David Harvey develops a theory of 'new imperialism'. It provides an important account of the relationship with historical imperialism and today (Harvey, 2003). Harvey explains that 'imperialism is a word that trips easily off the tongue' –the word has frequently been used in the anti-war movement, often simply as a synonym for war – 'it has such different meanings that it is difficult to use it without clarification as an analytical rather than a polemical term' (Harvey, 2003, 27). Therefore Harvey uses a definition specified as 'capitalist-imperialism', a contradictory combination of 'the politics of state and empire' and 'the molecular processes of capital accumulation in space and time' (Harvey, 2003, 27).

This notion of twin logics draws on and develops Giovanni Arrighi's conception of 'territorial' and 'capitalist' logics of power (Arrighi, 1994, 33). Harvey argues that a specifically capitalist form of imperialism:

> arises out of a dialectical relation between territorial and capitalistic logics of power. The two logics are distinctive and in no way reducible to each other, but they are tightly interwoven. They may be construed as internal relations of each other. But outcomes can vary substantially over space and time.
>
> (Harvey, 2003, 183)

This understanding of imperialism as the result of two contradictory and competing logics is the crucial to Harvey's theory.

Accumulation by dispossession is one of the key concepts developed by Harvey. It draws on the work of Rosa Luxemburg in *The Accumulation of Capital* and the idea that capital accumulation has a dual character (Luxemburg, 2003). The first is the extraction of surplus value, an economic exchange between capitalist and wage labourer, while the second 'concerns the relations between capitalism and the non-capitalist modes of production', appearing as a 'tangle of political violence and contests of power' (Harvey, 2003, 140). Instead of seeing the two as separate historical phases, Luxemburg views them as 'organically linked'. The analysis that Luxemburg put forward is based upon a theory of underconsumption as the explanation of economic crisis, which has been critiqued (Brewer, 1990; Bleaney, 1976). However, despite this Harvey argues that Luxemburg's conceptualisation remains useful. The 'idea that capitalism must perpetually have something "outside of itself" in order to stabilize itself is worthy of scrutiny, particularly as it echoes Hegel's conception … of an inner dialectic of capitalism forcing it to seek solutions external to itself' (Harvey, 2003, 140). There are therefore two 'outsides' that capitalism can utilise: firstly a 'pre-existing outside'. This could involve a non-capitalist 'outside', for example the seizure of land from indigenous communities. It could also involve a sector within capitalism that could be proletarianised, for example Margaret Thatcher's privatisation of state-owned companies and social housing in Britain. Secondly, capitalism can seek to 'actively manufacture it' (Harvey, 2003, 140).

This argument has similarities with Hannah Arendt's theory of imperialism. Her analysis saw the economic depression of the 1860s and 1870s in Britain as the impetus for a new form of imperialism. She argues that the bourgeois realised

> for the first time that the original sin of simple robbery, which centuries ago had made possible 'the original accumulation of capital' [see: Marx, 1867, p. 915] and had started all further accumulation, had eventually to be repeated lest the motor of accumulation suddenly die down.
>
> (Arendt, 1968, 28)

It is therefore not possible to 'relegate accumulation based upon predation, fraud, and violence to an "original stage" that is considered no longer relevant or, as with Luxemburg, as being somehow 'outside of' capitalism as a closed system' (Harvey, 2003, 144).

To make sense of the exploitation, inequality, and global divisions of labour today, it is therefore necessary to return to what has previously been called primitive accumulation. This concept was defined by Marx as the process of development of capitalism that involved:

> The discovery of gold and silver in America, the extirpation, enslavement and entombment in mines of the indigenous population of the continent, the beginning of the conquest and plunder of India, and the conversion of Africa into a preserve for the commercial hunting of blackskins, are all things which characterize the dawn of the era of capitalist production.
>
> (Marx, 1867, 915)

The argument that Harvey uses is that these are not only present at the 'dawn' but play an important role in contemporary capitalist production too. Therefore, the terminology is updated from primitive accumulation to the more appropriate 'accumulation by dispossession'.

This draws attention to the importance of space in the economy (Harvey, 1989; 2007). As Henri Lefebvre has argued, capitalism survives through the production of space (Lefebvre, 1991). Harvey goes beyond this, arguing that that the understanding needs to go beyond this. Both Lenin's and Luxemburg's theories of imperialism sought to understand the crises of capitalism. Harvey's approach introduces the idea of a 'spatio-temporal fix' as a response to the contradictions of capital accumulation. This is defined in the context of imperialism:

> A certain portion of the total capital is literally fixed in and on the land in some physical form for a relatively long period of time (depending on its economic and physical lifetime). Some social expenditures (such as public education or a healthcare system) also become territorialized and rendered geographically immobile through state commitments. The spatio-temporal 'fix', on the other hand, is a metaphor for a particular kind of solution to capitalist crises through temporal deferral and geographical expansion.
>
> (Harvey, 2003, 115)

The lack of opportunities for capital to make a profit in one place or time results in shifts to others.

This provides a useful framework for understanding how the dynamics of imperialism continue today. However, Harvey's analysis has also drawn criticism. For example, Harvey's interpretation of the importance of the 'molecular processes of capital accumulation' has drawn criticism (Harvey, 2003, 26). Firstly, Robert Brenner argues that the analysis fails to take into account the historic role of imperialism, instead reducing 'the great wave of European territorial expansion and its geopolitical consequences is understood, virtually in its entirety, in terms of the imperatives of capital accumulation' (Brenner, 2006, 86). Secondly, Ben Fine argues that the extension of Marx's 'primitive accumulation' removes the aim of the 'act to create wage-labour where previously it was absent', something crucial for understanding many of the transformations that have reshaped the contemporary world (Fine, 2006, 143).

Despite this criticisms, Harvey's understanding of the importance of space for capitalism, as well as connecting it to the longer specific histories of imperialism, provides an important explanation for how the current global division of labour came into being – as well as how it is maintained. There is only a Global North because there is a Global South. High-income countries did not come into being in isolation.

RESHAPING GLOBAL EMPLOYMENT

One of the major trends that has reshaped global employment in recent decades is the shift in manufacturing employment from the Global North to the Global South. In particular, since the 1980s, manufacturing has grown rapidly in China. With the entry of both global and private capital into export processing zones in China, it was 'transformed into a market economy under the wave of industrial relocation from advanced capitalist countries to the global South' (Ngai, 2016, 5). Computers, electronics, machinery, and other manufactured goods increasingly started to be made in China and the Global South, primarily for export to the Global North, as well as for emerging local markets.

The national and regional differences in employment provided an important opportunity for capital to take advantage. This global movement of production was part of the search for a new 'spatial fix' for capital (Harvey, 2003). In the case of China, the appeal for capital was clear, there is a very large potential workforce. Moreover, the costs of employing Chinese workers can be 'as low as one-sixth that of Mexico and one-fortieth that of the US' (Ngai, 2016, 6). These dynamics can be seen in the establishment of large export processing zones like that in Shenzhen, China. An often-cited example is the Foxconn factories that produce components for consumer electronics, like the iPhone (Chan et al., 2020). The increase in forms of employment in the Global North that rely on laptops, smartphones, and digital infrastructure would not be possible without workers in these factories.

The movement of workplaces – whether large factories, mines, or offices – from one place to another is an expensive undertaking. However, there has been a rising trend of not only the relocation of factories to the Global South, but also the outsourcing of parts of a company. The most famous example of this kind of business process outsourcing can be found with call centres (Sallaz, 2019). In Britain, the much talked about example is customer service for finance and telecommunication companies being outsourced to call centres based in India (Taylor and Bain, 2004; 2005). The growth of this process is due to a combination of both 'transationalization' and the 'liberalization' of regulations that opened up the 'reach of capital via global markets into correspondingly open national markets' (D'Costa, 2005, 34).

There has also been the development of a wider IT industry that is focused on working with business customers in the Global North and particularly the USA. This is a kind of 'transnational interactive services industry', which has important implications for the kinds of employment available in countries like India (Murphy, 2011, 1). One example is that call centre workers in India have to perform 'authenticity' for customers on the other side of the world, often for people they will not meet or places they will not get to visit (Mirchandani, 2012). This also might mean working at times that suit the customer, rather than worker, as 'firms routinely reroute calls from UK to Indian centres when UK operators are busy, at night or weekends, or when overtime rates apply at home' (Glucksmann, 2004, 807). This relocation of call centres often follows historical roots of imperialism which have resulted in shared language. For example, call centres in India for British customers, in the Philippines for the USA, and Latin America for Spain and Portugal.

This is a transformation of employment through the creation of new kinds of labour markets. At the simplest, labour markets involve the interaction of people selling their labour-power (workers) with people buying labour-power (employers). Like other markets, there can be differing supply and demand within a labour market. Often labour economists focus on labour markets to try and understand different outcomes, whether that be levels of employment, wages paid, and so on. There are often spatial constraints on labour markets. Workers may not want to move to access another workplace, or they may have ties to a particular place. As David Harvey notes, 'labor-power has to go home every night' (Harvey, 1989, 19). These processes of globalisation and outsourcing provide a way for employers to either directly or indirectly access new labour markets. This could involve setting up new workplaces like factories or outsourcing parts of their businesses. The aim of doing this has often been to access workers who can be paid less, thus lowering costs.

The most extreme examples of this can be found with crowdsourcing. The term refers to 'the act of a company or institution taking a function once performed by employees and outsourcing it to an undefined (and generally large) network of people in the form of an open call' (Howe, 2006). The application of this to outsourcing employment has the potential to access a global labour market, so long as workers have access to the internet. The establishment of platforms (which will be discussed in more detail in chapter four) provides a way for companies to access this form of outsourcing with very little outlay of initial costs. For example, platforms like Amazon Mechanical Turk or Upwork offer companies the opportunity to break down larger projects into micro tasks that can then be distributed to a large number of individual workers who do not need to be in contact with each other. This process of breaking employment up – both for the larger project and for the worker themselves – is often discussed as working in the 'gig economy' (Woodcock and Graham, 2019). Across the globe, there are now 'millions' of workers in 'low-income countries like Kenya who can use online work to transcend some of their local labour market's constraints' (Graham, 2015). This, as some have argued, is leading to the creation of a new 'planetary labour market' (Graham and Anwar, 2019). However, it is worth noting that the model of this 'platform work' (discussed more in detail in chapter four) is not employment, but instead presented as self-employment.

UNEMPLOYMENT

Over both time and place there have been significant variations in what kinds of work count as employment. For example, if the current global employment rate is 55.8%, then 44.2% of people are unemployed. In practice, this would mean that 207.2 million are unemployed (ILO, 2022). Without context, this could make it sound like over half of people are working in steady employment, while just under half of people are doing nothing. Of course, in practice the boundaries between employed/unemployed and what counts as work are much more blurred. For example, as can be seen in Table 2.5 there are a range of different forms of unemployment.

There are differences when these are examined by income groups of countries. For each of the categories (with explanations in Table 2.6), there are changes that can be observed. The clearest of these is that 'time-related unemployment', 'NEETs', and 'underutilized labour' are much higher in low-income than high-income countries. There are more workers who are not finding employment, or enough employment, in lower-income countries. The other notable feature of this table is the range of different indicators of unemployment, demonstrating that the reality for workers is much more complicated than the employed/unemployed distinction.

Table 2.5 Unemployment by Income Groups 2019

	Not in Labour Force	Potential Labour Force	Unemployment	Time-related under-employment	NEETs	Total Underutilized Labour
Low-income countries	32.7%	5.3%	4.9%	15.9%	21.3%	20.2%
Lower-middle income countries	45.2%	3.3%	5.1%	9.4%	25.7%	11.8%
Upper-middle income countries	34.5%	3.2%	6%	10.6%	19.9%	13.8%
High-income countries	39%	2.7%	4.8%	7.9%	10.4%	10.3%

Source: Adapted from ILO, 2022

Table 2.6 Unemployment Status Definitions

Unemployment	'Persons in unemployment are defined as all those of working age who were not in employment, carried out activities to seek employment during a specified recent period AND were currently available to take up employment given a job opportunity.'
Not in Labour Force	'Persons outside the labour force comprise all persons of working age who, during the specified reference period, were not in the labour force (that is, were not employed or unemployed). The working age population is commonly defined as persons aged 15 years and older, but this varies from country to country. In addition to using a minimum age threshold, certain countries also apply a maximum age limit.'
Potential Labour Force	'Persons in the potential labour force are those of working age that are not in employment, but that satisfied only one of the two conditions needed to be classified as unemployed: carried out activities to seek employment during a specified recent period, OR were currently available to take up employment given a job opportunity. Members of the potential labour force are not part of the labour force, but composes, together with the labour force, the extended labour force.'
Time-related underemployment	'Persons in employment who are willing and available to increase their working time (for production within the SNA production boundary) and worked fewer hours than a specified time threshold during the reference period. It signals inadequate employment.'
NEETs	'This provides a measure of youth aged 15-24 who are outside the educational system, not in training and not in employment, and thus serves as a broader measure of potential youth labour market entrants than youth unemployment, since it also includes young persons outside the labour force not in education or training. This indicator is a better measure of the current universe of potential youth labour market entrants compared to the youth inactivity rate, as the latter includes those youth who are not in the labour force and are in education, and thus cannot be considered currently available for work.'
Total Underutilized Labour	'The sum of unemployement, the potential labour force and time-related underemployment gives total labour underutilization, a composite measure of labour market slack.'

Source: Adapted from ILO, 2022

INFORMAL WORK

Beyond this employed/unemployed distinction there are important experiences of work that need to be considered. The difficulty is that often work that falls outside of these boundaries is difficult to measure. Informal work, for example, covers a range of unregistered economic activities. The informal economy – sometimes called the shadow economy – can therefore be defined as the 'market-based production of goods and services, whether legal or illegal, that escapes detection in the official estimates of GDP' (Smith, 1994, 18). For workers, this means 'those economic activities and the income derived from them that circumvent or otherwise

Table 2.7 Taxonomy of Types of Underground Economic Activities

Type of activity	Monetary transactions		Non-monetary transactions	
ILLEGAL ACTIVITIES	Trade in stolen goods; drug dealing and manufacturing; prostitution; gambling; smuggling; fraud; human trafficking, drug trafficking, and weapon trafficking.		Barter of drugs, stolen goods, smuggling, etc.; producing or growing drugs for own use; theft.	
LEGAL ACTIVITIES	Tax evasion	Tax avoidance	Tax evasion	Tax avoidance
	Unreported income from self-employment; wages, salaries, and assets from unreported work related to legal services and goods	Employee discounts; fringe benefits	Barter of legal services and goods	All do-it-yourself work and neighbour help

Source: Adapted from Schneider, 2005, 114

avoid government regulation, taxation or observation' (Dell'Anno, 2003, 4). In some cases, this is seen as an aberration or otherwise marginal part of the economy. However, in many countries, this can make up a substantial part of the overall economic activities.

Given the nature of many of these activities, it should not be surprising that measurement would be difficult. Many of these activities are deliberately hidden from official documentation, whether through tax evasion or illegality. There are, however, some estimations of how large these 'shadow economies' are in different countries. For these estimates of the 158 countries over 1991 to 2015, the average size of the shadow economy varies significantly. The lowest three are Switzerland with 7.2%, the United States with 8.3%, and Austria with 8.9%. The highest three are Zimbabwe with 60.6%, Bolivia with 62.3%, and Georgia at 64.87%. The average across all countries is 31.8%. For reference, the United Kingdom is 11.1% (Medina and Schneider, 2018, 69–76).

The existence of informal and shadow activities may therefore represent a third or more of the total on average. There are clear advantages to employers choosing to operate in this way. It avoids the payment of a range of taxes, both in income but also others like sales or value added. Employers do not have to pay social security contributions, which in some jurisdictions represents a substantial saving in costs. Similarly, by operating outside of regulation, they do not have to observe minimum wages or other standards. Overall, it reduces the administrative burden of complying with officials and authorities (Schneider, 2005).

While some of these activities may be criminal enterprises or other forms of large-scale organisation, much of this is also informal forms of work. For example, small-scale trading, forms of self-employment, or other types of casual or irregular work. It is often labour-intensive and is unregulated as it operates outside any existing forms of labour market regulation. In many countries in the Global South this kind of informal work is the majority.

UNPAID LABOUR

The third important distinction to make is that of unpaid labour. One of the defining features of employment is that it involves a 'mutually advantageous' relationship (Wertheimer, 1996, 14). This means payment for the labour involved in the transaction. However, when examining these different forms of paid employment – or ways in which people are trying to find work – there is a risk of missing the importance of other kinds of labour and work. The gendered history of capitalism and employment has often ignored unpaid work and labour. All forms of employment rely on work, both that of people employed but also of a wide range of invisible forms of work. Unpaid labour is vital to all modes of production (Vogel, 1995). There is no employment, no labour markets, no workers, without the unpaid labour that first produces workers and then reproduces them every day (Federici, 1975).

Alongside the other divisions of labour generated by capitalism, there has also been a sexual division of labour: wage labour for men and domestic labour for women. The history of gendered history of capitalism is more complex in practice than this (as can be seen in the previous chapter), but the creation of the household under capitalism continues to shape dynamics of work. Mariarosa Dalla Costa and Selma James argued that 'where women are concerned, their labor appears to be a personal service outside of capital' (Dalla Costa and James, 1971, 10). Rather than being paid for their labour, it was not treated as work that could be carried out for a wage. It is worth pointing out how similar many of these activities are to those carried out in employment. Yet, unlike the productivity increases developed in industry with the application of technology and machinery:

> the same cannot be said of housework; to the extent that she must *in isolation* procreate, raise and be responsible for children, a high mechanization of domestic chores doesn't free any time for the woman. She is always on duty, for the machine doesn't exist that makes and minds children.
>
> (Dalla Costa and James, 1971, 11)

However, this work allowed the worker (and in this context, often a man) to go and work in the factory, while women were left to carry out domestic work in the home.

This domestic labour, housework, and care are vital for employment. This can be understood as 'social reproduction' (Bhattacharya, 2017). This refers to the unpaid labour that is necessary to reproduce society. This is both in the direct sense of reproducing the next generation of workers as well as reproducing society itself each day. Workers have to first be born and raised, as well as socialised, taught, and cared for before they can go to work. After a day at work, workers need to prepare for the next day, including managing a household, preparing and eating meals, washing clothes, and so on.

This previous gendered division of labour is increasingly being replaced by both men and women working, although the entry of even more women into the labour market has not removed the distinction. Working women are often expected to continue domestic work as a 'second shift' after the first shift at work, unlike men (Hochschild, 1989). Other forms of employment have grown, including a service sector in which 'many reproductive activities formerly performed within the family' have become 'services available on the market: food preparation; laundry work; house cleaning; care for children, elderly people, the disabled, and the ill' (Marazzi 2011, 75). This work, although now paid, remains gendered and often racialised. In some contexts, like Britain and the USA, this also involves migrant workers moving from the Global South to work as cleaners, nannies, and carers.

A GLOBAL VIEW OF EMPLOYMENT

The purpose of this chapter has been to introduce the idea of a global division of labour in understanding employment. Whether you are trying to understand how employment works in Britain or any other country, the social relations of employment in one location are increasingly shaped by global dynamics and trends. As noted at the beginning of this chapter, it would be very difficult to give an accurate global picture of employment, given the huge diversity of experiences that this involves in practice. However, by looking at some of the key trends, particularly those between different income groups of countries, it is possible to sketch out some of the differences.

Workers in different countries enter employment under different circumstances. For example, they may be employees, holding relatively stable forms of employment for payment. They may be part of family businesses which involve relationships not found in other forms of work. They may work on their own account, with less clear employment relationships, or even be employers themselves. The kinds of work, conditions, and pay vary significantly between countries.

An important part of making sense of these differences is the historic and continuing role of imperialism. The world is an increasingly unequal place, riven with conflict, exploitation, and the extraction of value and resources from the Global North to the Global South. These relationships are not separate from employment but shape it in important ways. This can be seen in the movement of some kinds of work, whether that be manufacturing or outsourcing of service work, and the movement of commodities through global supply networks.

These differences in employment can also be further complicated by examining how unemployment (often seen as the opposite of work) operates in different contexts. Much of the experience of employment is different to the 'standard employment relationship', instead taking in informal kinds of work and other activities that are not considered to be work like domestic labour. Rather than being atypical or away from the standard, this suggests that the experiences in Global North countries like Britain or the USA are in the minority.

The aim of this chapter was to provide the wider global context in which employment is situated. While the focus, as discussed earlier, is predominantly on Britain, this global picture is important to remember. The forms of employment in Britain today are only possible because of the history of imperialism and exploitation that have shaped the global divisions of labour.

REFERENCES

Arendt, H. (1968) *Imperialism: Part Two of the Origins of Totalitarianism*, New York, Harcourt Publishers.

Arrighi, G. (1994) *The Long Twentieth Century: Money, Power, and the Origin of our Times*, London, Verso.

Bhattacharya, T. (ed.) (2017) *Social Reproduction Theory: Remapping Class, Recentering Oppression*, London, Pluto Press.

Bleaney, M. (1976) *Underconsumption Theories: History and Critical Analysis*, London, Lawrence and Wishart.

Brenner, R. (2006) 'What Is, and What Is Not, Imperialism?', *Historical Materialism*, vol. 14, no. 4, pp. 79–105.

Brewer, A. (1990) *Marxist Theories of Imperialism: A Critical Survey*, London, Routledge.

Chan, J., Selden, M. and Pun, N. (2020) *Dying for an iPhone: Apple, Foxconn and the lives of China's workers*, London, Pluto Press.

Dalla Costa, M. and James, S. (1971) *The Power of Women and the Subversion of the Community*, Brooklyn, NY, Pétroleuse Press.

D'Costa, A. P. (2005) *The Long March to Capitalism: Embourgeoisment, Internationalisation and Industrial Transformation in India*, Basingstoke, Palgrave MacMillan.

Dell'Anno, R. (2003) *Estimating the shadow economy in Italy: A structural equation approach*, Economic Working Paper No. 2003-07, Department of Economics, The University of Aarhus.

Englert, S. (2022) *Settler colonialism: an introduction*, FireWorks, London, Pluto Press.

Federici, S. (1975) 'Wages against housework', in Malos, E. (ed), *The Politics of Housework*, New York, New Clarion Press, pp. 187–194.

Fine, B. (2006) 'Debating the "New" Imperialism', *Historical Materialism*, vol. 14, no. 4, pp. 133–156.

Glucksmann, M.A. (2004) 'Call configurations: varieties of call centre and divisions of labour', *Work, Employment & Society*, vol. 18, no. 4, pp. 795–811.

Graham, M. (2015) 'Digital work signals a global race to the bottom', *Sci Dev Net* [Online]. Available at www.scidev.net/global/icts/opinion/digital-work-signals-global-race-bottom.html.

Graham, M. and Anwar, M.A. (2019) 'The Global Gig Economy: Towards a Planetary Labour Market?', *First Monday*, vol. 24, no. 4 [Online]. DOI: 10.5210/fm.v24i4.9913.

Harvey, D. (1989) *The Urban Experience*, Oxford, Blackwell.

Harvey, D. (2003) *The New Imperialism*, Oxford, Oxford University Press.

Harvey, D. (2007) *A Brief History of Neoliberalism*, Oxford, Oxford University Press.

Hochschild, A.R. (1989) *The Second Shift: Working Families and the Revolution at Home*, New York, Penguin.

Howe, J. (2006) 'The Rise of Crowdsourcing', Wired [Online]. Available at www.wired.com/2006/06/crowds/.

ILO (2022) *World Employment and Social Outlook* [Online]. Available at www.ilo.org/wesodata/.

Lefebvre, H. (1991) *The Production of Space*, Oxford, Wiley-Blackwell.

Lenin, V. I. (1965) *Imperialism, the highest stage of capitalism*, Peking, Progress.

Luxemburg, R. (2003) *The Accumulation of Capital*, Abingdon, Routledge.

Marazzi, C. (2011) *Capital and Affects: the politics of the language economy*, Semiotext(e) foreign agents series, Los Angeles, CA, Semiotext(e).

Marx, K. (1867) Capital: A Critique of Political Economy Vol. 1, 1976, London, Penguin Books.

Medina, L. and Schneider, F. (2018) *Shadow Economies Around the World: What Did We Learn Over the Last 20 Years?*, IMF Working Papers, International Monetary Fund.

Mirchandani, K. (2012) *Phone Clones: Authenticity Work in the Transnational Service Economy*, London, ILR Press.

Murphy, J. (2011) 'Indian call centre workers: Vanguard of a global middle class?', *Work, Employment and Society*, vol. 25, no. 3, pp. 417–33.

Ngai, P. (2016) *Labour in China: Post-Socialist Transformation*, Cambridge, Polity.

Sallaz, J.F. (2019) *Lives on the Line: How the Philippines became the World's Call Centre Capital*, Oxford, Oxford University Press.

Schneider, F. (2005) 'The Size of Shadow Economies in 145 Countries from 1999 to 2003', *he Brown Journal of World Affairs*, vol. 11, no. 2, pp. 113–129.

Smith, P. (1994) *Assessing the size of the underground economy: the statistics canada perspective.*, National Accounts & Environment Division, Statistics Canada.

Taylor, P. and Bain, P. (2004) 'Call Centre Offshoring to India: The Revenge of History?', *Labour and Industry*, vol. 14, no. 3, pp. 15–38.

Taylor, P. and Bain, P. (2005) '"India calling to the far away towns": the call centre labour process and globalization', *Work, Employment and Society*, vol. 19, no. 2, pp. 261–282.

The World Bank (2022) *World Bank Country and Lending Groups* [Online]. Available at https://datah elpdesk.worldbank.org/knowledgebase/articles/906519-world-bank-country-and-lending-groups.

Vogel, L. (1995) *Woman Questions: Essays for a Materialist Feminism*, New York, NY, Routledge.

Wertheimer, A. (1996) *Exploitation*, Princeton, NJ, Princeton University Press.

Woodcock, J. and Graham, M. (2019) *The Gig Economy: A Critical Introduction*, Cambridge, Polity.

CHAPTER 3

THE MANAGEMENT OF WORK

One of the most important defining aspects of employment is that it is managed. Unlike the many other forms of work that exist, the employment relationship involves the management of that work. Despite the importance of this, the definition of management can be hard to pin down in practice. For example, try asking a manager what they actually do. The answer is often complicated: they 'manage' people, processes, and maybe other things at work.

The Oxford English Dictionary defines 'management, n.' as:

1.   a. Organization, supervision, or direction; the application of skill or care in the manipulation, use, treatment, or control (of a thing or person), or in the conduct of something...

   b. Originally: the working or cultivation of land. Later also: the maintenance and control of a forest, environment, nature reserve, etc. In extended use: the conservation and encouragement of natural resources such as game, fish, wildlife, etc. Frequently with modifying word...

6.   a. Governing body of an organization or business, regarded collectively; the group of employees which administers and controls a business or industry, as opposed to the labour force. Also: the group of people which runs a theatre, concert hall, club, etc...

7.   *Medicine.* The care of a patient or treatment of a disease or condition; (also) the coordinated course of action determined for this purpose...

8.   a. The responsibility for and control of the resources of a company, department, or other organization. Frequently as the second element in compounds.

   b. management by exception n. a technique of business management in which a manager only intervenes in operations under his or her control when exceptional or problematic situations arise.

   c. management by objectives n. a technique of business management in which the performance of each manager is assessed and improved by setting regular objectives.

(Oxford English Dictionary, 2022a)

We can see here some of the different meanings of management in practice, some of which are beyond work, referring to nature or other organisations. The origin of the word, first documented in the 1500s, has the following etymological roots:

> In the 17th and 18th centuries the development of meaning was influenced by association with Middle French, French †*mesnagement* (French *ménagement*) household economy (1551), measure in one's actions (17th cent.), consideration and constraint toward others (1665): compare French *ménager* (see ... manage, v. to take charge of, control, or direct (a household, institution, business, state, etc).
>
> (Oxford English Dictionary, 2022a)

The use of the word 'control' here is important. The roots of the word 'manage' make this clearer. It comes from the Italian *maneggaire* meant 'to handle (1298–1309), to be able to use skilfully, to manage, direct or exercise a horse'. To 'manage' is therefore 'to control (a person or animal); to exert one's authority or rule over' (Oxford English Dictionary, 2022b). Control is a theme we will return to throughout this chapter.

There have also been a range of definitions of management put forward in the literature:

> 'Management is the art of knowing what you want to do and then seeing that it is done in the best and cheapest way' (Taylor, 1967).

DOI: 10.4324/9781003279907-4

'To manage is to forecast and plan, to organise, to command, to coordinate and to control' (Fayol, 1916).

'Management is concerned with the systematic organisation of economic resources and its task is to make these resources productive' (Drucker, 1954).

'Managing is an operational process initially best dissected by analysing the managerial functions ... The five essential managerial functions (are): planning, organising, staffing, directing and leading, and controlling' (Koontz and O'Donnell, 1959).

'Management is the art of securing maximum results with minimum efforts so as to secure maximum prosperity for employer and employee and give the public the best possible service' (Mee, 1963).

'Five areas of management constitute the essence of proactive performance in our chaotic world: (1) an obsession with responsiveness to customers, (2) constant innovation in all areas of the firm, (3) partnership – the wholesale participation of and gain sharing with all people connected with the organisation, (4) leadership that loves change (instead of fighting it) and instils and shares an inspiring vision, and (5) control by means of simple support systems aimed at measuring the "right stuff" for today's environment' (Peters, 1987).

As can be seen from the shifting definitions of management over time, it begins with a relatively straightforward directive: profit maximisation, but then develops into a wider set of issues.

HUMAN RESOURCE MANAGEMENT

The dominant way of theorising how employment is managed today is Human Resource Management. At business schools across the world, there are Human Resource Management (HRM) courses, as well as HR departments across many companies. HRM develops from the longer history of employment and management discussed in chapter one, particularly with Taylorism and scientific management (Taylor, 1967).

As Henri Fayol argued, there are five classic functions of management in the context of employment, shown in Table 3.1 (Fayol, 1917).

Table 3.1 Five Functions of Management

Function	Description
To forecast and plan	'According to Fayol, forecasting ("prévoyance" in French) involves analysing the future and drawing up a plan of action (Pugh and Hickson, 2007). Arguably, managers engage in an element of forecasting, analysis of the environment and appraising the microenvironment of the organisation through strategic planning (Hill and McShane, 2008). The globalised knowledge economy and the presence of ubiquitous change and competition make forecasting, planning and strategising key managerial activities.'
To organise	'Fayol believed that an organisation's structure was important, as it facilitated the optimum conduct of its business activities (Pugh and Hickson, 2007). In contemporary terms, to organise requires managers to implement an appropriate infrastructure, which will optimise the organisation's systems, resources, procedures, processes and services and enable knowledge to be disseminated to those who need it, when they need it (Stonehouse and Pemberton, 1999). Furthermore, organising also incorporates resourcing the organisation with appropriate human, financial and material resources.'

Table 3.1 (Cont.)

Function	Description
To command	'In his original writing, Fayol used the term "command" to illustrate a manager's responsibility to lead and direct employees towards the achievement of organisational goals and strategies (Pugh and Hickson, 2007). "To command" may sound rather draconian these days, but remember, Fayol espoused his theory during a period of widespread industrialisation and managers had a firm grip on how the organisation was run (classical school). They may not have exercised the participative management styles many of us are familiar with today. In 21st Century terms, Hill and McShane (2008) use the word leadership, instead of command, to describe the process of directing, influencing and motivating individuals to work towards the achievement of organisational goals and objectives (Yukl and Lespringer, 2005). Moreover, Fayol advocated that managers should develop a thorough knowledge of their employees (Pugh and Hickson, 2007), which, arguably, can be by engendering a positive psychological contract that engages employees with their jobs and the organisation.'
To co-ordinate	'Fayol suggested that managers should bind together, unify and harmonise all the organisation's activities and efforts. This translates to contemporary management practice, insofar as managers are responsible for ensuring that all the organisation's business activities are co-ordinated to maintain synergy and symbiosis between its functions and processes and internal and external contexts. Importantly, this includes the input-conversion-output process. Hill and McShane (2008) posit that co-ordination has now been subsumed into the function of organising, as there is synergy between them.'
To control	'Fayol recognised the importance of control within an organisation and espoused that it ensures "everything occurs in conformity with established rules and expressed command" (Pugh and Hickson, 2007, 100). Using 21st Century parlance, control is one of the most important responsibilities of a manager and involves exercising appropriate leadership to ensure that everything is working according to plan and within budget, set timescales and allocated resources. Control works hand in hand with planning, strategising and organising (Hill and McShane, 2008) and seeks to facilitate the alignment of individual and organisational performance. In their role as controllers, managers must ensure that appropriate contingencies are in place to buffer deviations from original plans and swiftly deal with system anomalies, to prevent disruption to any of the organisation's business activities. Control could be seen as the underpinning function of management because without it, carrying out the other four functions would be extremely difficult.'

Source: Adapted from McLean, 2011

While each of these are important for managing employment, controlling is a key part of the process. Control was an obsession of Taylorism and remains the answer to the problem of the indeterminacy of labour-power that is purchased in the employment relationship. The 'essence of control is action which adjusts operations to pre-determined standards, and its basis is information in the hands of managers' (Sherwin, 1956, 46). This means establishing standards and objectives, then finding ways to measure the actual performance of workers, comparing the results with objectives and standards, and taking corrective action if needed.

46 The Management of Work

Control can take different forms in practice. For example, Table 3.2 shows a range of different kinds of control.

In practice, this means there are a variety of different forms that control has, and can take on, in the workplace. For example, in Table 3.3, forms of control are outlined in factories, call centres, and in gig economy platforms.

Control can also involve different aspects of consent and coercion (Burawoy, 1979). At the most basic, 'consent' involves management winning approval for the decisions being made, whereas 'coercion' means effectively enforcing those decisions. What is, of course, missing from the discussion so far is workers' responses. This is where the choice of 'human resource' in HRM can sometimes be perplexing. People in the employment relationship are much more than just 'human resources'. As discussed in the first chapter, people bring more to the employment

Table 3.2 Management Control Systems

Elements	Description	Components
Planning	'Ex-ante form of control (Flamholtz et al., 1985); first it sets out the goals of the functional areas of the organisation thereby directing effort and behaviour; second, it provides the standards to be achieved in relation to the goal, making clear the level of effort and behaviour expected; third, it enables congruence by aligning goals across the functional areas of an organisation, thereby controlling the activities of groups and individuals.'	'Action planning—goals and actions for the immediate future, usually a 12-month period, are established; has a tactical focus. Long-range planning— the goals and actions for the medium and long run are established; has a more strategic focus.'
Cybernetic	'There are five characteristics of cybernetic control (Green and Welsh, 1988). First, there are measures that enable quantification of an underlying phenomenon, activity or system. Second, there are standards of performance or targets to be met. Third, there is a feedback process that enables comparison of the outcome of the activities with the standard. This variance analysis arising from the feedback is the fourth aspect of cybernetic control systems. Fifth is the ability to modify the system's behaviour or underlying activities.'	'*Budgets* (Hansen et al., 2003; Bunce et al., 1995), *Financial measures* (Ittner and Larcker, 1998), *Non-financial measures* (Ittner and Larcker, 1998), *Hybrids* that contain both financial and non-financial measures such as the Balanced Scorecard (BSC) (Kaplan and Norton, 1992, 1996b, 1996a, 2001b, 2001a; Malina and Selto, 2001; Ittner and Larcker, 1998; Greenwood, 1981; Kondrasuk, 1981)'
Reward / compensation	'Motivating and increasing the performance of individuals and groups through attaching rewards to control effort direction, effort duration, and effort intensity.'	'Attaching rewards and or compensation to achievement of goals (Bonner and Sprinkle, 2002; Flamholtz et al., 1985)'

Table 3.2 (Cont.)

Elements	Description	Components
Administrative	'Administrative control systems are those that direct employee behaviour through the organizing of individuals (organisation design and structure), the monitoring of behaviour and who employees are made accountable to for their behaviour (governance); and through the process of specifying how tasks or behaviours are to be performed or not performed (policies and procedures) (Simons, 1987).'	'*Organisational design and structure* (Alvesson and Kärreman, 2004; Abernethy and Chua, 1996; Emmanuel et al., 1990; Otley and Berry, 1980), *Governance structures* within the firm (Abernethy and Chua, 1996), *Procedures and policies* (Macintosh and Daft, 1987; Simons, 1987)'
Culture	'The values, beliefs and social norms which are established influence employees behaviour (Pratt and Beaulieu, 1992; Dent, 1991; Birnberg and Snodgrass, 1988).'	'*Value-based controls* (Simons, 1995), *Clan controls* (Ouchi, 1979), *Symbols* (Schein, 1997)'

Source: Adapted from Malmi and Brown, 2008

Table 3.3 Systems of Control

	Factory	Call Centre	Transport platform
Direction	Taylorist separation of conception and execution of work, workers given specific instructions. Assembly line automatically sets central pace	Separation of conception and execution of work with scripting. Automatic dialling of calls increases pace	Separation of conception and execution of overall work on platform. Workers receive direction through smartphone, but can have discretion with route choices
Evaluation	Supervisors assess the labour process on the factory floor, quality assurance of outputs	Quantitative metrics from electronic supervision, qualitative evaluation by supervisors	Automated evaluation of the labour process with quantitative metrics. Customer evaluation in some cases
Discipline	Supervisors encourage performance, bonuses can be used to increase output. Sanctions for poor performance	Supervisors encourage performance, bonuses used to increase output. Sanctions for missing targets	Use of bonuses to encourage engagement at peak times. Automated interventions based on automated evaluation ('deactivations')

Source: Woodcock, 2022

relationship than just their labour-power, and often want to get more out of it than just payment for their time. The history of employment, as discussed, is both a history of management control and worker resistance. There are many responses that workers can have to control, including acceptance and acquiescence, refusal and resistance, and much more in between. The sections that follow will examine the different ways that management theory has attempted to implement that control in different ways.

RECRUITMENT AND SELECTION

The process of management begins before the worker is employed. While we often focus on management in the workplace, deciding who to recruit and why is also an important management function. However, in practice finding potential workers is not a straightforward process:

> Recruitment may be thought of as a positive process of generating a 'pool' of candidates by reaching the 'right' audience, suitable to fill the vacancy while selection can be seen as a more negative process of choosing or 'picking' from among that 'pool'"the most suitable candidate(s), both able and willing to fill the vacancy.

> (Leopold, 2002, 54)

Recruitment therefore aims to attract qualified candidates, with different opportunities for intervention. For example, managers can try to bring the job opening to the attention of potential candidates, then influence whether they apply for the job, then maintain interest until a job offer is made, and finally try to influence whether a job offer is accepted. Each of these may sound relatively straightforward, but in practice it means doing this within a labour market with other competing organisations and offers.

Recruitment requires engaging with labour markets. Theoretically, this means a very large recruitment pool. However, workers are limited in where they can work. As David Harvey argued, 'labor-power has to go home every night' (Harvey, 1989, 19). Workers are place-based and often have ties whether through family, friendships, or preferences. The reality is that labour markets are more constrained and limited. Nevertheless, external labour markets provide access to a wider pool of potential candidates beyond the organisation. This can bring in new ideas and perspectives to an organisation, as well as matching skills of employees to the job. It may involve traditional methods of advertising job vacancies, for example in newspapers or trade press. Advertising can be handled by agencies or headhunters, collaboration with educational institutions, other forms of media, conferences, or networks like LinkedIn.

Internal labour markets can also be used for recruitment to roles. Rather than seeking candidates beyond the organisation, this could mean internal promotions. Although organisations that focus on this are still required to hire externally at the lowest levels in order to have employees to promote. Existing employees can then apply for vacancies, which lowers the cost of recruitment. There are potential benefits for this approach, including motivating and engaging current employees. Training may prove to be a better investment that open recruitment. For managers, this means that employees may be less likely to leave, promoted employees already know the organisation so require less induction. It may also be that there is less risk as employees have already been through a selection process and managers know more about the candidates through their existing practice and performance. This does have potential risks in that it restricts the pool of candidates and can make it harder to implement change.

The 'selection' part of this process is about trying to find out which candidates to hire. There are a range of academic approaches to this. One is the Attraction-Selection-Attrition (ASA) model (Schneider et al., 1995; Schneider, 1987). This involves three parts:

- Attraction. Individuals are attracted to firms with similarly attitudes, personalities, and values.

- Selection. Organisations select on compatibility. This often means choosing people who are similar.

- Attrition. If people do not fit within an organisation, then they leave.

ASA is therefore:

a person-based framework for understanding organizational behavior. In ASA the organization (its structure, process, and culture) is hypothesized to be a function of the personalities of the people there; the organization is the outcome of the founders and top management of organizations and the people subsequently attracted to, selected by, and retained there.

(Schneider et al., 1995, 761)

The model is shaped by the founders, who then determine the culture and behaviours. The attraction and selection of similar people leads to a homogenous culture within an organisation. As those who do not fit leave, this culture becomes strengthened. This build on the idea that 'people make the place' and therefore determine organisational behaviour (Schneider, 1987).

A homogenous organisation can create management problems. For example, if everyone is broadly the same, this could make change difficult. There is already a shared understanding of of what is being done – as well as what might need to be done. This can lead to problems of 'group think'. This might limit the potential for responding to changes outside of an organisation (or even realising that change is needed). This also raises questions about the use of personality within a workplace setting.

A key part of understanding this is what 'fit' means within an organisation. One way of conceptualising this is 'person-organisation fit'. This compares the compatibility between individuals and organisations. In Figure 3.1, 'supplementary fit' (with arrow 'a') is the relationship between the characteristics of an organisation and a person. When there is a fit between these, there is a supplementary fit. The model also explores how the relationships between organisations and individuals involves the supply and demand of different things during employment. These are shaped by the characteristics of either the organisation or person, but involve distinct elements which could lead to fit or misfit. In particular, this attempts to draw out the different resources supplied and demanded by both organisations and people. When organisational supplies meet employees' demands, 'needs-supplies' fit is achieved (with arrow 'b'). Similarly, 'demands-abilities fit' is achieved when employee supplies (including KSAs – Knowledges, Skills, and Abilities) meet organisational demands. These are both forms of 'complementary fit' (Kristof, 1996, 4).

These different forms of fit are a key part of the selection process in many organisations. Supplementary fit happens when a worker 'supplements, embellishes, or possesses characteristics which are similar to other individuals' in an environment or organisation (Muchinsky and Monahan, 1987, 269). This is a version of fit that we have probably come across in many other contexts – finding a home within a group with shared ideas, norms, and behaviours. Complementary fit, on the other hand, happens when a worker's characteristics 'make whole' the environment (Muchinsky and Monahan, 1987, 271). This involves adding a needed part to an organisation. This might be a particular strength or KSA. Finding a fit in an organisation can increase trust (Boon and den Hartog, 2011). When taken together with the ASA theory, there is a model in which workers are attracted to organisations in which they perceive a level of person-organisation fit (Gregory et al., 2010).

Recruitment therefore requires careful consideration of both who is being recruited and selected, as well as what the role being filled is. When searching for a new job in most industries, it is usual to find an advert that lists details about the job. These mostly contain the following: job title, location, grade or level, who they are responsible to/for, duties of the job, and working

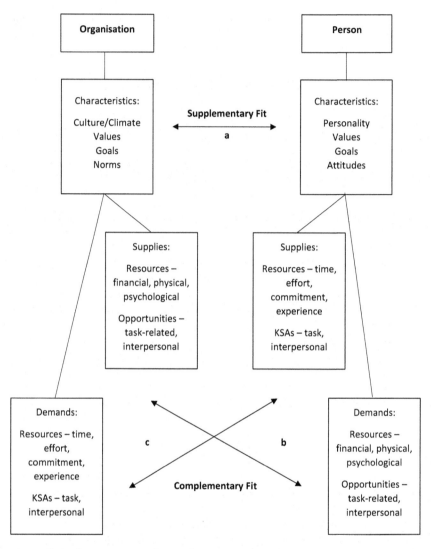

FIGURE 3.1 **Complementary and Supplementary Fit**

Source: Adapted from Kristof, 1996

conditions. In some cases, this may specify the KSAs needed for the role – and the education, training, qualifications, and experience that are needed to have those KSAs. In white-collar work (which Human Resource Management often focuses on) these are so-called 'competencies'. These tend to be soft skills of various kinds, including aspects like communication, teamwork, leadership, problem-solving, relationship management, and so on. This can be seen in Table 3.4, that provides an example of a competency-based person specification for a recruitment specialist.

As these different attempts to explain and develop these processes show, there is much more to recruitment and selection than putting out adverts for a job opening. Of course, this part of the process is still important. In practice, the process now involves more steps than it used to. The core of the recruitment process is the application form, the interview, and references. Each of these provide information to the manager about the suitability of a candidate for selection. The

Table 3.4 Competency-based Person Specification for a Recruitment Specialist

1. Knowledge of:
   - All aspects of Recruitment
   - Sources of recruits
   - Different media for use in recruiting
   - Relevant test instruments
2. Skills in:
   - Interviewing techniques
   - Test administration
   - Role analysis
3. Behavioural competencies:
   - Able to relate well to others and use interpersonal skills to achieve desired objectives
   - Able to influence the behaviour and decisions of people on matters concerning recruitment and other HR or individual issues
   - Able to cope with change, to be flexible, and handle uncertainty
   - Able to make sense of issues, identify and solve problems and 'think on one's feet'
   - Focus on achieving results
   - Able to maintain appropriately directed energy and stamina, to exercise self-control, and learn new behaviours
   - Able to communicate well, orally and on paper

Source: Adapted from Armstrong, 2020, 314

application form allows for initial screening of candidates, with an opportunity to sift out those who do not meet the requirements. The interview process provides an opportunity to both meet the candidate and also gather further information or test their responses. The references provide a check on previous employment and how they have performed in other roles. In some industries and job types, there are other aspects that have become common. For example, the use of personality tests.

If working in a job that requires specific skills, there may be tests on work samples. For example, completing a coding test or submitting an example of written work. Assessment centres use exercises that attempt to simulate parts of the jobs and test candidates' ability to complete them. These can involve a range of tasks, including role-playing and group exercises. Instead of an interview which involves one candidate, this can involve a group setting which is more like the environment in which the candidate may be working.

It is also important to note that there is a darker side to the process of recruitment. Choosing who to employ is also about choosing who not to employ. While this is always part of selection, there are instances in which this goes much further. For example, in the UK an organisation called Consulting Association operated an illegal blacklist in the construction industry for decades. They compiled a database of information on building workers, including employment history, political views, trade union membership, health, and personal relationships. Building companies could check the files before employing a worker. This provided a way for companies to avoid employing those they saw as potential troublemakers. There are stories of workers being added to the blacklist after raising concerns about health and safety on building sites. Those who could not find work had no knowledge of the secret blacklist until it was uncovered by campaigning workers as part of the Blacklist Support Group and an investigative journalist (Smith and Chamberlain, 2015). In the court trial that followed, further information about collaboration with state agencies emerged. The judge ruled in favour of the blacklisted workers, including ordering £35 million in compensation (Evans, 2019).

PAY AND REWARDS

Pay, rewards, compensation, remuneration, whatever term is used, is a key reason why workers enter into employment. The choice of how much to pay and the way it is paid is an important lever that management has at work. It is also an important component for workers. People choose to work for the income and it has major implications for quality of life. For an organisation, it is often a major component of costs – although this does vary by industry.

Pay played an important role in Taylor's *Principles of Scientific Management*. As Taylor recounts in a story about Schmidt, the pig iron handler, pay could be used to increase output. As he asks Schmidt:

> What I want to find out is whether you are a high-priced man or one of these cheap fellows here. What I want to find out is whether you want to earn $1.85 a day or whether you are satisfied with $1.15, just the same as all those cheap fellows are getting.
>
> (Taylor, 1967, 41)

Schmidt responds that he wants to be a 'high-priced man' and agrees to load more pig iron – from 12 to 47 tons in a day – for the higher wage. However, for Taylor the motivation of more money was not only for greater output. He argued that:

> If you are a high-priced man, you will do exactly as this man tells you tomorrow, from morning till night. When he tells you to pick up a pig and walk, you pick it up and you walk, when he tells you to sit down and rest, you sit down. You do that right straight through the day. And what's more, no back talk. Now a high-priced man does just what he's told to do, and no talk back.
>
> (Taylor, 1967, 42)

The trade-off for more pay is to not 'talk back' to the manager. Thus, the 'high-priced man' is selling more than just the additional output, but also submitting to the authority of the manager. Reflecting on this, Taylor notes that:

> This seems to be rather rough talk. And indeed it would be if applied to an educated mechanic, or even an intelligent laborer. With a man of the mentally sluggish type of Schmidt it is appropriate and not unkind, since it is effective in fixing his attention on the high wages which he wants and away from what, if it were called to his attention, he probably would consider impossibly hard work.
>
> (Taylor, 1967, 43)

Taylor's patronising explanation reveals an important component of pay: that it can be used to distract from the both the quantity and quality of work.

A similar use of pay can be found with Henry Ford's use of the five-dollar day (Ford, 1926). In 1914, The Ford Motor Company announced that it would be doubling wages to five dollars a day. The developments in the moving assembly line from 1913 had reduced the time required to make a Model T from 12.5 hours to 93 minutes. This massive reduction in time also involved deskilling of the workforce, reducing the complexity of the tasks involved. Workers responded to the new conditions of work, with a turnover rate of 370%. The announcement of the five-dollar day led to thousands of people arriving at the gates of the Ford factory in Detroit. Those who were hired found that the five-dollar day was not as simple as advertised. Workers still earned the $2.30 they had previously, but could be awarded a bonus of $2.70. This involved work-related requirements, but also paternalistic demands for workers to abstain from alcohol, have clean homes, and save money. Ford even employed inspectors to check up on workers' home lives (Anderson, 2014).

Max Weber proposed a different kind of payment system. Organisations should instead be rationally formalised, separate to the individuals involved within them. Instead of paying different rates based on outputs, members of a bureaucracy should be paid a fixed amount depending on their job and its place within the hierarchy (Weber, 1930).

Barnard argued that organisations were a form of cooperative system. Each person within an organisation needed to be induced to make contributions towards a common goal. Pay was an important inducement, but other factors like power and status could also be used (Barnard, 1938). Simon developed this further by making the distinction, first, between the decision to join and participate in an organisation, and second, with the decisions that participants make on behalf of an organisation (Simon, 1947). These two contributions started a focus in the literature on employee motivation. Pay as part of what makes individuals join and remain in organisations, as well as how their behaviours within organisations can be influenced.

These ideas of motivation and pay were developed by three further sets of thinkers. The first is Maslow, famed for his 'hierarchy of needs' (Maslow, 1969). Although it is often presented as a pyramid, this was not how it was presented in the original work. The hierarchy of needs (see Table 3.5) sets forth different levels of needs. The theory claims that for motivation for the next stage to arise, the previous stage must be satisfied (from the bottom of the table upwards). The goal is to reach the highest levels of self-fulfilment.

Within Maslow's hierarchy of needs, pay allows workers to meet their basic needs. Pay can cover physiological needs, as well as possibly provide financial safety. Given the hierarchy of needs, the implication is that once pay has risen above the necessary level to meet these needs, the satisfaction of other needs will take priority over pay.

The connection of motivation and pay was further developed by Herzberg. Rather than understanding satisfaction and dissatisfaction as ends of a spectrum, he reconceptualised these as independent factors (Herzberg, 1966). Some factors may cause satisfaction, while others may create dissatisfaction. This two-factor theory of job satisfaction was based on interviews with engineers and accountants:

> Briefly, we asked our respondents to describe periods in their lives when they were exceedingly happy and unhappy with their jobs. Each respondent gave as many 'sequences of events' as he could that met certain criteria—including a marked change in feeling, a beginning, and an end, and contained some substantive description other than feelings and interpretations ... The proposed hypothesis appears verified. The factors on the right that led to satisfaction (achievement, intrinsic interest in the work, responsibility, and advancement) are mostly unipolar; that is, they contribute

Table 3.5 Hierarchy of Needs

Transcendence	A broader category that includes spiritual needs as well as altruism	Self-fulfilment needs
Self-actualisation	The need to achieve full potential	
Aesthetic	The need for beauty or aesthetic pleasures	Psychological needs
Cognitive	The need for meaning and information, which can be expressed in a desire to learn	
Esteem	The need for self-respect and respect from others	
Belonging and love	The need for forms of social acceptance within groups, both large and small	
Safety	The need for stability, including health and personal, emotional, and financial security	Basic needs
Physiological	The basic biological needs for survival, including air, food, water, clothing, shelter, and so on	

Source: Adapted from Maslow, 1969

very little to job dissatisfaction. Conversely, the dis-satisfiers (company policy and administrative practices, supervision, interpersonal relationships, working conditions, and salary) contribute very little to job satisfaction.

(Herzberg, 1964, 4)

Herzberg therefore distinguished between 'motivators', that is factors that are intrinsic to the job including recognition, achievement, and personal growth, and 'hygiene factors' that are extrinsic to the job including pay, conditions, and so on, that do not provide higher motivation, but the absence of them can lead to dissatisfaction. The term hygiene is used to signal that these are a kind of maintenance factor. The different combinations of these can lead to a range of outcomes. First, high hygiene and high motivation, in which employees are highly motivated and content. Second, high hygiene and low motivation, in which employees are content with the job but not highly motivated. Third, low hygiene and high motivation, in which employees are highly motivated by the job, but the conditions need improvement. Fourth, low hygiene and low motivation, a clearly negative outcome (Herzberg, 1964). In this context, pay is an important hygiene factor, meaning that it could be a powerful source of dissatisfaction, but could not be a source of satisfaction on its own.

Both Maslow and Herzberg have been criticised for the lack of empirical evidence from workplaces (Rynes et al., 2004). Despite the differences in intrinsic and extrinsic motivation, pay is an important – indeed often the first – motivator for employment. There is an important difference in how pay is handled in practice within organisations. Pay is about more than just the salary or wages that are paid to a worker. While this is, of course, very important, there are a range of other incentives that shape how workers are paid. The fixed amounts that are paid regularly to workers often comprise the largest part of pay. However, historically and in particular industries, paying for workers' housing, costs, or other commodities can take up a large part of this.

Before moving on to pay directly, there are also two kinds of benefits or perks that can be given in employment. Non-risk benefits are often pre-tax expenditure. This means that in cases where additional pay may involve higher taxes, they can involve significant savings if the organisation purchases these benefits rather than the worker. Similarly, if they are purchased in bulk by the organisation, further savings can be made. Examples include company cars, transport, meals, housing, childcare, loans, education, or other discounts. Risk benefits involve the purchasing of risk-based commodities like pensions and insurance. There are similar benefits to non-risk benefits, but further savings can be made from pooling risks and the economies of scale. In some cases, there may be pressures from the state or other institutions to provide these. In Britain, for example, all employers have to provide pension provisions.

Another form, albeit one that is limited to specific industries and job roles, is equity plans. Stock options or employee stock ownership plans are an attempt to align the interests of employees and shareholders. Like other benefits, they can involve substantial tax savings. Stock options are often used to try and retain highly paid employees, while stock ownership plans allow a way for workers to buy stock with pre-tax income or with discounts.

In terms of understanding how pay is determined, there are a variety of theories in the literature. In classical economics, the level of pay is determined by the market through supply and demand. Pay levels are therefore set at the price at which labour transactions clear in the market. This imagines a free market in which information is readily available and workers can move easily from one employer to another. However, in practice markets do not work like that. There are many instances in which the 'market' does not operate in a normal way. One example is the payment of what are called 'efficiency wages' (Akerlof and Yellen, 1986). Some organisations pay higher wages than the going market rate. This can be seen both at the higher and lower levels of wages. For example, many organisations choose to pay above the minimum wage for jobs roles that others choose to keep at that level. Henry Ford's five-dollar day discussed earlier is an important historical example.

There are a number of arguments made in the literature for why this might happen. One example is understanding the role of deferred wages. Organisations may gain efficiencies from employing people long term. There may be a lower salary at first, during the time in which productivity is lower. However, as workers reach retirement age, they may have less productivity – while their wages would have grown over time. There may therefore be a wage less than productivity at first, while the wage is higher than productivity later in a career (Lazear, 1979). This highlights how efficiency wages can change depending on the internal labour market at different points. Another argument is that internal labour markets might operate as a form of tournament (Lazear and Rosen, 1981). For example, in professional firms, there is often a competitive promotion scheme, in which very large salary increases are not connected to productivity. For example, in accountancy, this may involve employees entering as accountants, then either becoming senior accountants or leaving. There is then a progression to managers and partners, which involve significant competition and salary increases. This is connected to the idea of deferred wages (Lazear and Gibbs, 2009), but is also used to motivate those at the entry level with the possibility of large rewards that outweigh productivity.

Another approach to this is equity theory (Adams, 1963; 1965). This starts from an understanding of the employment relationship as an exchange – drawing on the notions of contributions and inducements (Barnard, 1938). The theory proposes that employees compare their contributions and inducements ratio against others. This can lead to internal and external comparisons. If there is inequity, then workers can adjust their contribution (both up and down) to match the ratio of others. For example, if a worker sees that colleagues are contributing much less, they may well reduce their own contribution. This has important implications if there are substantial differences in wages within or between organisations. Wage dispersion involves difference in wage levels for workers doing the same jobs (Mortensen, 2003), while wage compression refers to there being little difference, regardless of experience or productivity (Lazear and Gibbs, 2009). Both of these are of concern for managers as they can result in problems. Wage dispersion can create problems for cooperation, for example, if one worker knows they are being paid less than another for the same role. Similarly, if there is wide wage dispersion across an organisation. There are often attempts to keep pay secret or prevent disclosure – despite this being illegal in many jurisdictions. Wage compression, on the other hand, can lead to workers leaving to get increased wages elsewhere. There can also be instances of wage inversion, in which newer workers earn more than experienced workers, exacerbating the problem for managers further.

Broadly speaking, there are two different ways that managers determine pay in practice. First, pay for the time spent at work. This may be related to the job or task, status, skills, or seniority. Job-related pay might involve pay scales set by an institution. For example, universities in the UK often have salary bands with steps for pay increments within them. It may also be influenced by other institutional factors. For example, the minimum wage levels set by the state or legislation on equal pay. It might be influenced by collective bargaining or other pressures, like the independently set living wages.

Second, pay for the results of the work or output. This can involve piece rates, commission, or pay for performance, either for the individual, team, or organisation. There are a range of different ways to refer to this, for example, incentives, performance-related pay, pay for performance, pay by results, variable or contingent pay. The theory behind paying in this way is deeply influenced by the principle-agent problem (Jensen and Meckling, 1976). The problem involves the starting point that an 'agent' is hired to do something on behalf of a 'principal'. The outcome for the principal depends on the agent's behaviour – how much effort they put in or risks they take. The principal has a problem in that it is difficult to effectively monitor the agent's behaviours. The agent pursues behaviours that are not costly to them (avoiding risk), while avoiding behaviours that are costly to them (in terms of effort). This outcome prevents the principal from achieving what they want.

The proposed solution to the principal-agent problem is ensuring that incentives are used to align the interests of the agent to those of the principal. This takes inspiration from expectancy theory (Vroom, 1964). This assumes that behaviours in the employment relationship can be motivated if there is a positive correlation between effort and performance, that performance will result in desirable rewards, and that the reward has value attached that makes the effort worthwhile. There is evidence that pay for performance can work in this way in varying contexts (Lazear, 2000; Fernie and Metcalf, 1999).

There are also importance instances in which performance-related pay may not work in practice. This can be the result of breaches of expectancy theory. For example, there may be no possibility of increasing effort in the first place. There may be a disconnection between effort and performance, whether due to weak goal setting, failures of coordination, or lack of skills. The link between performance and reward may also be broken, perhaps due to a failure of effective measurement of performance, or through lack of availability of rewards, or other management failure. The rewards may not be valued by workers, they could be in conflict with other motivational factors, or the motivation of managers in given the reward may be distrusted.

Each of these managerial practices illustrates ways to set pay that are covered by either institutional factors or ways to try and motivate workers. However, there remains an important issue with pay that is not often discussed in terms of management practices: wage theft. Often, employment is discussed as a contract in which both parties come together and meet their requirements. However, for many workers, unpaid wages can be a part of the experience of employment. For example, the Unpaid Britain (Clark and Herman, 2017) project found that £1.2 billion in wages and £1.5 billion in holiday pay are stolen from workers every year. As Nick Clark explained:

> It has not been easy to find accurate data on the true scale of failure to pay wages in this country and I fear that this is the tip of the iceberg in terms of painting a realistic picture of unpaid Britain. One of the problems is that there is no official data on non-payment. Not paying wages is a civil rather than a criminal offence which means there are no crime statistics. Our interim findings demonstrate that there is a desperate need for improved workers' protection and better guidance on their rights and how these can be enforced. With an uncertain Brexit around the corner there has never been a more important time to safeguard, protect and enhance workers' rights.
>
> (Clark, 2017)

This suggests that not only is paying workers a strategy, with all the different forms that can involved, but also that not paying workers is a systematic managerial strategy.

RETENTION, ENGAGEMENT, AND TURNOVER

The chapter has so far addressed the way workers are employed and how much they receive for their work. This section looks at the ways managers try to retain and engage workers, as well as reasons that workers choose to leave employment.

Employment is a voluntary agreement. This, of course, discounts the need for workers to find and keep employment to have access to a wage to buy things. The individual employment relationship between worker and organisation is ultimately temporary – whether because workers choose to leave or eventually retire. For management, this leaving of workers is often described as 'turnover'. That turnover can be voluntary or involuntary, or be avoidable or unavoidable.

Retention is the way that managers try to ensure that workers stay in the employment relationship. This is important because high levels of turnover can be incredibly harmful to an organisation. The process of recruitment and selection of new employees is costly, both in time and resources. Workers need to adapt to a new job, leading to much lower productivity than a workforce that has been in place. When workers leave this takes knowledge and expertise away from an organisation, as well as potentially losing relationships, both internally but also with customers and clients. However, there will always be some level of turnover inside an organisation.

Turnover can be understood in terms of push and pull factors. Push factors are those that repel a worker from an organisation. This could be due to dissatisfaction with the organisation or the work. Pull factors attract workers from outside an organisation, including the attractiveness of rival employers. Holtom et al. provide a model for how voluntary turnover can be understood, see Figure 3.2 (Holtom et al., 2008, 244).

The turnover model draws together existing research to try and understand voluntary turnover – that is, why workers choose to leave an organisation. It covers a wide range of factors that can help to explain why turnover happens.

As Table 3.6 shows, job dissatisfaction is not the only reason for turnover in organisations. It focuses on a range of different factors, that claims to explain the majority of reasons why workers leave. It starts from whether or not there is a shock ('yes', Paths 1–3; 'no', Paths 4a and 4b). A shock can be positive or negative. It is 'a particular, jarring event that initiates the psychological analysis involved in quitting a job' (Lee et al., 1999, 451). This could include things like changes in marital state or unsolicited job offers. The 'script' refers to whether the worker has a plan of action that existed before the shock. An 'image violation' can take place when a worker's own values and goals no longer align with the organisation and can be connected to the shock. 'Satisfaction' refers to lower levels of satisfaction with the job. 'Search' involves the activities of looking for another job and comparing it to the existing one, while 'likely offer' refers to the possibility of being offered one of those alternatives (Lee et al., 1999, 451).

These different paths provide a way to examine different routes to voluntary turnover. For example, in Path 1, a worker experiences a shock, but they have an existing plan for how to deal with it. Image violation and job satisfaction are irrelevant for this path, and the worker leaves without considering either the possible alternatives or their own attachment to the organisation. Each of the other paths trace out other options for why people may leave. For example, Path 4b is the version most often considered for turnover. That low levels of job satisfaction lead to workers searching for alternatives and then leaving when they find them (Lee et al., 1999, 452). The importance of this is that it provides different moments and opportunities for managers to try and intervene to stop workers leaving. One solution to this is thinking about how management can ensure employee engagement. However, engagement is not straightforward. It is a combination of something created in an organisation and something that the employee brings to the organisation. Indeed, embeddedness in the organisation is a predictor of retention (Holtom and Inderrieden, 2006). It can therefore act as a buffer to the shocks discussed above. Therefore, many organisations develop retention plans that take these factors into account.

EMPLOYEE VOICE

The final part of this chapter considers how these approaches to management work in practice. The first thing to note is that workers are relatively absent from these theoretical discussions, other than as subjects to be acted upon or predicted by managers. However, unlike other resources in organisation, human resources come attached to people. People are complex and contradictory and bring much more to an organisation than just their time and skills. Human Resource Management often operates in a very different context to the history of employment

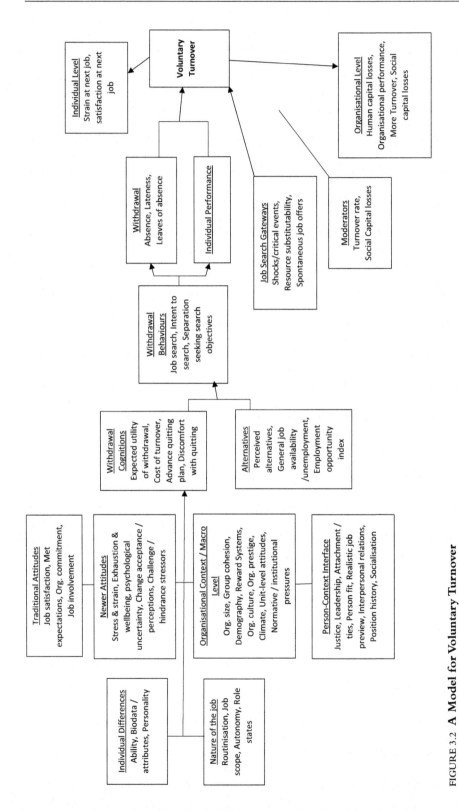

FIGURE 3.2 **A Model for Voluntary Turnover**

Source: Adapted from Holtom et al., 2008, 244

Table 3.6 The Unfolding Model of Voluntary Turnover

Path	Shock	Script	Image Violation	Satisfaction	Search and/ or evaluation of alternatives	Likely offer
1	Yes	Yes	Irrelevant	Irrelevant	No	No
2	Yes	No	Yes	Irrelevant	No	No
3	Yes	No	Yes	Low	Yes	Yes
4a	No	No	Yes	No	No	No
4b	No	No	Yes	No	Yes	Yes

Source: Adapted from Lee et al., 1996

discussed in chapter one. As noted elsewhere, the role of trade unions and other forms of workers' organisations is much smaller than it has been historically.

One way that Human Resource Management has sought to make sense of this is through the concept of 'employee voice'. This is a shift from the previous ways of thinking about employees having a say in their work. For example, in 1968 a Royal Commission report explained that 'collective bargaining is the most effective means of giving workers the right to representation in decisions affecting their working lives' (Donovan, 1968). There has been a range of academic debate on the reasons for, and the nature of, the changes from this trade union and collective bargaining approach to that of employee voice (Johnstone and Ackers, 2015). The CIPD defines it as follows:

> Employee voice is the means by which people communicate their views to their employer and influence matters that affect them at work. It helps to build open and trusting relationships between employers and their people which can lead to organisational success. For employers, effective voice contributes to building trust with employees, innovation, productivity and organisational improvement. For employees, self-expression in voice often results in feeling valued, increased job satisfaction, greater influence and better opportunities for development. Employee voice is important in creating inclusive and safe working environments too.
>
> (CIPD, 2021)

This definition is much more focused on the benefits of employee voice for the employer, as well as fitting it within broader managerial objectives. For example, the CIPD also breaks the definition down into two parts: 'organisational voice', which 'refers to the positive benefits that voice can bring to an organisation, for example, higher innovation. Some voice mechanisms, such as suggestion schemes, allow the organisation to benefit from employees' ideas'; and 'individual voice', which 'argues that voice is a fundamental right. It allows employees to be involved in decision-making and to express their concerns' (CIPD, 2021).

This idea of employee voice can come in many forms within different organisations. For example, in Table 3.7, Dundon et al. provide a range of different examples.

As can be seen in the table, there are a divergent range of forms that employee can take, as well as leading to quite different outcomes. In many cases, 'union collective representation has been *supplanted* by non-union voice in new workplaces and, where union voice persists in older workplaces, it has been *supplemented* by non-union voice' (Gomez et al., 2010, 398).

Despite the complementary role that employee voice can have within existing trade union practices, it is important to note, 'for some commentators independent unions are the only source of genuine voice' (Benson, 2000, 453). Practitioners can also have quite different understandings of employee voice. For example, Unipart's group HRD John Greatrex, noted that 'The phrase

Table 3.7 The Meaning and Articulation of Employee Voice

Voice as:	Purpose and articulation of voice	Mechanisms and practice for voice	Range of outcomes
Articulation of individual dissatisfaction	To rectify a problem with management or prevent deterioration in relations	Complaint to line manager; grievance procedure; speak-up programme	Exit – loyalty
Expression of collective organisation	To provide a countervailing source of power to management	Union recognition; collective bargaining; industrial action	Partnership – de-recognition
Contribution to management decision-making	To seek improvements in work organisation, quality, and productivity	Upward problem-solving groups; quality circles; suggestion schemes; attitude surveys; self-managed teams	Identity and commitment – disillusionment and apathy; improved performance
Demonstration of mutuality and co-operative relations	To achieve long-term viability for the organisation and its employees	Partnership agreements; joint consultative committees; work councils	Significant influence over management – marginalisation and sweetheart deals

Source: Dundon et al., 2004, 1152

employee voice per se isn't that useful as it means so many different things to different groups', while Unions 21 director Becky Wright explains that 'If we ask people what they think of collective voice they'd respond "what the hell is that?" And even those of us that understand it don't have an everyday answer' (quoted in Sharp, 2018). Regardless of this, finding ways to listen to workers' voices – whether these are mediated through a union, alternative methods, or heard through strikes or walkouts – management is always about interpersonal relationships, and these have to play a role in the process. The debate is not only about workers' voices, as these clearly (or audibly) exist, but whether or not they are listened to and what the response is.

MANAGEMENT IN PRACTICE

The employment relationship necessarily entails different interests as it brings together the employer and the employee. The principal-agent problem takes this as a starting point and much of the research on pay attempts to find ways to use rewards to align the interests within the employment relationship.

When considering Human Resource Management, it is often developed inside, and concerned with the interests of, the organisation. These approaches are the latest attempt to achieve what Taylor was trying to do. While on the surface they may seem like standard practices in many organisations, they are about the articulation of power, attempting yet again to try and control the labour process in the employment relationship. This means questions of ethics and judgement constantly come up in any instance in which management is attempted.

Table 3.8 RadHR Principles

Principle	Explanation
Anti-Oppressive	The world is already full of oppression. Our ways of organising—our policies, processes and practices—should be actively counteracting the white supremacy, patriarchy, classism, ableism, homophobia and transphobia experienced by many people in the wider world. As should the ways we engage with each other as a community across this site.
Radical	Oppression plays out on many levels: in wider society; in our group practices; and in our individual behaviours (often without us realising). This can make it really hard to challenge effectively—and sometimes even hard to see! In order to live our values, we need to be committed to push for change on all these levels, even—and especially—when doing so pits us against some of those dominant power structures, or forces us to challenge our own positions.
Collaborative	The question of how to really live our values is far too big for any of us to answer on our own! We need each other if we are going to figure out alternatives to the kinds of oppression that have dominated management / HR / organisational thinking for so long.
Transparent	To collaborate, we need to be able to share what we've got and what we've learned with others walking similar paths. There can be a vulnerability in sharing our learnings—especially when we're not 100% sure of what we know (which we never can be with this sort of work)! RadHR aims to create spaces where we can build the trust needed to share effectively with one another.
Messy	Organising in ways that radically shift existing power structures and oppressions is never going to be neat and tidy. Or comfortable. If it is, we're probably not changing that much. So instead of trying to avoid discomfort, uncertainty and untidiness, let's embrace the mess!

Source: RadHR, 2022

There are alternative ways of trying to understand management, including academic approaches like Critical Management Studies. Similarly, there have been approaches in practice that have tried to do things differently. For example, RadHR is 'about practically applying anti-oppressive ideas to how social change organisations and workplaces organise internally. It offers alternatives to off-the-shelf HR policies and processes, which tend to replicate the very oppressions that our organisations strive to challenge' (RadHR, 2022). Their policies begin from a different starting point to many of the theories discussed in this chapter. They are based on the principles outlined in Table 3.8.

They provide examples of policies and procedures that can be used in practice in organisations. For example, 'how to write a radical grievance or disciplinary policy', 'parent and carer staff support', or 'how to do radical safeguarding' (RadHR, 2022).

The other key issue of management in practice is that it often operates within organisational constraints. In many business schools, teaching is delivered through the use of case studies, like those found in the *Harvard Business Review*. These are often designed to show up bad management practice and offer the opportunity to put forward a theoretically informed solution to solve the problem of the case study. However, just as people are complex, so are many of the concrete situations in which management works in practice. A key driver of what practices can be implemented is cost. This means that many of the HR practices we find out in the world are often the cheapest, rather than being the most developed or theoretically informed.

REFERENCES

Abernethy, M.A. and Chua, W. (1996) 'Field study of control system "Redesign": the impact of institutional process on strategic choice', *Contemporary Accounting Research*, vol. 13, no. 2, pp. 569–606.

Adams, J.S. (1963) 'Towards an understanding of inequity', *Journal of Abnormal and Social Psychology*, vol. 67, no. 5, pp. 422–436.

Adams, J.S. (1965) 'Inequity in social exchange', *Advances in Experimental Social Psychology*, vol. 2, pp. 267–299.

Akerlof, G. and Yellen, J. (1986) *Efficiency Wage Models of the Labor Market*, Cambridge, Cambridge University Press.

Alvesson, M. and Kärreman, D. (2004) 'Interfaces of control. Technocratic and socio-ideological control in a global management consultancy firm', *Accounting, Organizations and Society*, vol. 29, no. 3–4, pp. 423–444 [Online]. DOI: 10.1016/S0361-3682(03)00034-5.

Anderson, M. (2014) *Ford's Five-Dollar Day* [Online]. Available at www.thehenryford.org/explore/blog/fords-five-dollar-day/.

Armstrong, M. (2020) *Armstrong's Handbook of Human Resource Management Practice*, 15th edn, London, Kogan Page Limited.

Barnard, C.I. (1938) *The Functions of the Executive*, Cambridge, MA, Harvard University Press.

Benson, J. (2000) 'Employee Voice in Union and Non-union Australian Workplaces', *British Journal of Industrial Relations*, vol. 38, no. 3, pp. 453–9.

Birnberg, J.G. and Snodgrass, C. (1988) 'Culture and control: A field study', *Accounting, Organizations and Society*, vol. 13, no. 5, pp. 447–464 [Online]. DOI: 10.1016/0361-3682(88)90016-5.

Bonner, S.E. and Sprinkle, G.B. (2002) 'The effects of monetary incentives on effort and task performance: theories, evidence, and a framework for research', *Accounting, Organizations and Society*, vol. 27, no. 4–5, pp. 303–345 [Online]. DOI: 10.1016/S0361-3682(01)00052-6.

Boon, C. and den Hartog, D.N. (2011) 'Human resource management, Person-Environment Fit, and trust', in Searle, R.H. and Skinner, D. (eds), *Trust and human resource management*, Cheltenham, Edward Elgar Publishing Limited, pp. 109–121.

Bunce, P., Fraser, R. and Woodcock, L. (1995) 'Advanced budgeting: a journey to advanced management systems', *Management Accounting Research*, vol. 6, no. 3, pp. 253–265 [Online]. DOI: 10.1006/mare.1995.1017.

Burawoy, M. (1979) *Manufacturing Consent*, Chicago, IL, University of Chicago Press.

CIPD (2021) *Employee Voice* [Online]. Available at www.cipd.co.uk/knowledge/fundamentals/relations/communication/voice-factsheet.

Clark, N. (2017) *Unpaid Britain*, Trust for London [Online]. Available at www.trustforlondon.org.uk/publications/unpaid-britain/.

Clark, N. and Herman, E. (2017) *Unpaid Britain: wage default in the British Labour Market*, Middlesex University.

Dent, J. F. (1991) 'Accounting and organizational cultures: A field study of the emergence of a new organizational reality', *Accounting, Organizations and Society*, vol. 16, no. 8, pp. 705–732 [Online]. DOI: 10.1016/0361-3682(91)90021-6.

Donovan, T.N. (1968) *Report of the Royal Commission on Trade Unions and Employers Associations*, HM Stationery Office.

Drucker, P. (1954) *The Practice of Management*, New York, Harper and Row.

Dundon, T., Wilkinson, A., Marchington, M. and Ackers, P. (2004) 'The meanings and purpose of employee voice', *The International Journal of Human Resource Management*, vol. 15, no. 6, pp. 1149–1170 [Online]. DOI: 10.1080/095851904100016773359.

Emmanuel, C., Otley, D. and Merchant, K. (1990) *Accounting for Management Control*, Padstow, Cornwall, Chapman and Hall.

Evans, R. (2019) '50 blacklisted trade unionists win £1.9m from building firms', *The Guardian*, 14th May [Online]. Available at www.theguardian.com/business/2019/may/14/50-blacklisted-trade-unionists-win-19m-from-building-firms.

Fayol, H. (1916) *General and Industrial Management*, Paris., Institute of Electrical and Electronics Engineering.

Fayol, H. (1917) *Administration industrielle et générale; prévoyance, organisation, commandement, coordination, controle*, Paris, H. Dunod et E. Pinat.

Fernie, S. and Metcalf, D. (1999) 'It's Not What You Pay it's the Way that You Pay it and that's What Gets Results: Jockeys' Pay and Performance', *Review of Labour Economics and Industrial Relations*, vol. 13, no. 2, pp. 385–411.

Flamholtz, E.G., Das, T.K. and Tsui, A.S. (1985) 'Toward an integrative framework of organizational control', *Accounting, Organizations and Society*, vol. 10, no. 1, pp. 35–50 [Online]. DOI: 10.1016/ 0361-3682(85)90030-3.

Ford, H. (1926) 'Mass Production', in Garvin, J. L. (ed), *The Encyclopedia britannica; a dictionary of arts, sciences, literature & general information*, 13th edn, London, The Encyclopædia britannica company, vol. 30.

Gomez, R., Bryson, A. and Willman, P. (2010) 'Voice in the Wilderness? The Shift From Union to Non-Union Voice in Britain', in Wilkinson, A., Gollan, P. J., Marchington, M., and Lewin, D. (eds), *The Oxford Handbook of Participation in Organizations*, 1st edn, Oxford University Press, pp. 383–406 [Online]. DOI: 10.1093/oxfordhb/9780199207268.003.0016 (Accessed 29 October 2022).

Green, S. and Welsh, M. (1988) 'Cybernetics and dependence: reframing the control concept', *Academy of Management Review*, vol. 13, no. 2, pp. 287–301.

Greenwood, R.C. (1981) 'Management by objectives: as developed by Peter Drucker, assisted by Harold Smiddy', *Academy of Management Review*, vol. 6, no. 2, pp. 225–231.

Gregory, B.T., Albritton, M.D. and Osmonbekov, T. (2010) 'The mediating role of psychological empowerment on the relationships between p–o fit, job satisfaction, and in-role performance', *Journal Business Psychology*, vol. 25, pp. 639–647.

Hansen, S., Otley, D. and Van der Stede, W. (2003) 'Practice developments in budgeting: an overview and research perspective', *Journal of Management Accounting Research*, vol. 15, pp. 95–116.

Harvey, D. (1989) *The Urban Experience*, Oxford, Blackwell.

Herzberg, F. (1964) 'The Motivation-Hygiene Concept and Problems of Manpower', *Personnel Administration*, vol. 27, pp. 3–7.

Herzberg, F. (1966) *Work and the Nature of Man*, New York, World Publishing Company.

Hill, C.W.L. and McShane, S. L. (2008) *Principles of management*, Boston, McGraw-Hill/Irwin.

Holtom, B.C. and Inderrieden, E. J. (2006) 'Integrating the Unfolding Model and Job Embeddedness Model to Better Understand Voluntary Turnover', *Journal of Managerial Issues*, vol. 18, no. 4, pp. 435–452.

Holtom, B.C., Mitchell, T.R., Lee, T.W. and Eberly, M.B. (2008) '5 Turnover and Retention Research: A Glance at the Past, a Closer Review of the Present, and a Venture into the Future', *Academy of Management Annals*, vol. 2, no. 1, pp. 231–274 [Online]. DOI: 10.5465/19416520802211552.

Ittner, C.D. and Larcker, D.F. (1998) 'Innovations in performance measurement: trends and research implications', *Journal of Management Accounting Research*, vol. 10, pp. 205–239.

Jensen, M.C. and Meckling, W.H. (1976) 'Theory of the firm: Managerial behavior, agency costs and ownership structure', *Journal of Financial Economics*, vol. 3, no. 4, pp. 305–360.

Johnstone, S. and Ackers, P. (eds) (2015) *Finding a voice at work? new perspectives on employment relations*, First edn, Oxford, Oxford University Press.

Kaplan, R. . and Norton, D.P. (1992) 'The balanced scorecard—measures that drive performance', *Harvard Business Review*, vol. 70 (January–February), pp. 71–79.

Kaplan, R.S. and Norton, D.P. (1996a) 'Using the Balanced Scorecard as a Strategic Management System', *Harvard Business Review*, vol. 74 (January–February), pp. 75–85.

Kaplan, R.S. and Norton, D.P. (1996b) *Translating Strategy into Action: The Balanced Scorecard*, Boston, Harvard Business Press.

Kaplan, R.S. and Norton, D.P. (2001a) *The Strategy-Focused Organization: How Balanced Scorecard Companies Thrive in the New Business Environment*, Boston, Harvard Business School Publishing Corporation.

Kaplan, R.S. and Norton, D.P. (2001b) 'Transforming the balanced scorecard from performance meas-
    urement to strategic management: Part 1', *Accounting Horizons*, vol. 15, no. 1, pp. 87–104.
Kondrasuk, J.N. (1981) 'Studies in MBO effectiveness', *Academy of Management Review*, vol. 6, no. 3,
    pp. 419–431.
Koontz, H. and O'Donnell, C. J. (1959) *Principles of Management: An Analysis of Managerial Functions*,
    New York, McGraw-Hill.
Kristof, A.L. (1996) 'Person-organization fit: An integrative review of its conceptualizations, measure-
    ment, and implications', *Personnel Psychology*, vol. 49, no. 1, pp. 1–49.
Lazear, E.P. (1979) 'Why Is There Mandatory Retirement?', *Journal of Political Economy*, vol. 87, no. 6,
    pp. 1261–1284.
Lazear, E.P. (2000) 'Performance Pay and Productivity', *American Economic Review*, vol. 90, no. 5,
    pp. 1346–1361.
Lazear, E.P. and Gibbs, M. (2009) *Personnel economics in practice*, 2nd edn, Hoboken, NJ, John Wiley
    & Sons.
Lazear, E. and Rosen, S. (1981) 'Rank-Order Tournaments as Optimum Labor Contracts', *Journal of
    Political Economy*, vol. 89, no. 5, pp. 841–64.
Lee, T.W., Mitchell, T.R., Holtom, B.C., McDaniel, L.S. and Hill, J.W. (1999) 'The Unfolding Model
    of Voluntary Turnover: A Replication and Extension', *Academy of Management Journal*, vol. 42, no. 4,
    pp. 450–462.
Lee, T.W., Mitchell, T.R., Wise, L. and Fireman, S. (1996) 'An Unfolding Model of Voluntary Employee
    Turnover', *Academy of Management Journal*, vol. 39, pp. 5–36.
Leopold, J. (ed) (2002) *Human resources in organisations*, 2nd print, Harlow, Pearson Education.
Macintosh, N. and Daft, R. (1987) 'Management control systems and departmental independencies: an
    empirical study', *Accounting Organizations and Society*, vol. 12, no. 1, pp. 23–28.
Malina, M. and Selto, F. (2001) 'Communicating and controlling strategy: an empirical study of the
    effectiveness of the balanced scorecard', *Journal of Management Accounting Research*, pp. 47–90.
Malmi, T. and Brown, D.A. (2008) 'Management control systems as a package—Opportunities,
    challenges and research directions', *Management Accounting Research*, vol. 19, no. 4, pp. 287–300
    [Online]. DOI: 10.1016/j.mar.2008.09.003.
Maslow, A.H. (1969) 'Theory Z', *Journal of Transpersonal Psychology*, vol. 1, no. 2, pp. 31–47.
McLean, J. (2011) 'Fayol – Standing the test of time', *British Journal of Administrative Management*,
    vol. 74, pp. 32–33.
Mee, J.F. (1963) *Management Thought in a Dynamic Economy*, New York, New York University Press.
Mortensen, D.T. (2003) *Wage Dispersion: Why Are Similar Workers Paid Differently?*, The MIT Press
    [Online]. DOI: 10.7551/mitpress/7147.001.0001 (Accessed 14 September 2022).
Muchinsky, P.M. and Monahan, C.J. (1987) 'What is person-environment congruence? Supplementary
    versus complementary models of fit.', *Journal of Vocational Behavior*, vol. 31, no. 3, pp. 268–277.
Otley, D.T. and Berry, A.J. (1980) 'Control, organisation and accounting', *Accounting, Organizations and
    Society*, vol. 5, no. 2, pp. 231–244 [Online]. DOI: 10.1016/0361-3682(80)90012-4.
Ouchi, W. (1979) 'A conceptual framework for the design of organizational control mechanisms',
    Management Science, vol. 25, no. 9, pp. 833–848.
Oxford English Dictionary (2022a) *management, n.* [Online]. Available at www.oed.com/view/Entry/
    113218.
Oxford English Dictionary (2022b) *manage, v.* [Online]. Available at www.oed.com/view/Entry/
    113210.
Peters, T. (1987) *Thriving on Chaos: Handbook for a Management Revolution*, New York, Alfred A. Knopf.
Pratt, J. and Beaulieu, P. (1992) 'Organizational culture in public accounting: size, technology, rank and
    functional area', *Accounting Organizations and Society*, vol. 17, pp. 667–689.
Pugh, D.S. and Hickson, D.J. (2007) *Writers on Organisations*, 6th edn, London, Penguin Books.
RadHR (2022) *RadHR* [Online]. Available at https://radhr.org/about/.

Rynes, S.L., Gerhart, B. and Minette, K.A. (2004) 'The importance of pay in employee motivation: discrepancies between what people say and what they do', *Human Resource Management*, vol. 43, no. 4, pp. 381–394.

Schein, E. (1997) *Organizational Culture and Leadership*, San Francisco, Jossey-Bass.

Schneider, B. (1987) 'The people make the place', *Personnel Psychology*, vol. 40, no. 3, pp. 437–453.

Schneider, B., Goldstein, H.W. and Smith, D.B. (1995) 'The ASA framework: An update', *Personnel Psychology*, vol. 48, no. 4, pp. 747–773.

Sharp, R. (2018) 'Breaking the Silence: Employee Voice', *HR Magazine* [Online]. Available at www.hrmagazine.co.uk/content/features/breaking-the-silence-employee-voice/

Sherwin, D.S. (1956) 'The Meaning of Control', *Dunn's Business Review and Modern Industry*, January.

Simon, H.A. (1947) *Administrative Behavior: a Study of Decision-Making Processes in Administrative Organization*, New York, The Macmillan Company.

Simons, R. (1987) 'Accounting control systems and business strategy: An empirical analysis', *Accounting, Organizations and Society*, vol. 12, no. 4, pp. 357–374 [Online]. DOI: 10.1016/0361-3682(87)90024-9.

Simons, R. (1995) *Levers of Control*, Boston, Harvard University Press.

Smith, D. and Chamberlain, P. (2015) *Blacklisted: the secret war between big business and union activist*, Oxford, New Internationalist.

Stonehouse, G.H. and Pemberton, J.D. (1999) 'Learning and knowledge management in the intelligent organisation', *Participation and Empowerment: An International Journal*, vol. 7, no. 5, pp. 131–144.

Taylor, F.W. (1967) *The Principles of Scientific Management*, New York, Norton.

Vroom, V.H. (1964) *Work and motivation*, New York, Wiley.

Weber, M. (1930) *The Protestant Ethic and the Spirit of Capitalism*, London, Unwin Hyman.

Woodcock, J. (2022) 'Artificial intelligence at work: The problem of managerial control from call centers to transport platforms', *Frontiers in Artificial Intelligence*, vol. 5 [Online]. DOI: 10.3389/frai.2022.888817 (Accessed 28 October 2022).

Yukl, G. and Lespringer, R. (2005) 'Why Integrating the Leading and Managing Roles is Essential for Organisational Effectiveness', *Organisational Dynamics*, vol. 34, no. 4, pp. 361–75.

CHAPTER 4

KEY DYNAMICS OF CONTEMPORARY EMPLOYMENT

In this chapter, the book turns to contemporary debates on work and employment. First, we will examine state regulation and employment rights; second, the public sector and the state as employer; third, post-industrial employment and service work; fourth, emotional and affective labour; fifth, precarious work; sixth, platforms and the gig economy; and seventh, trade union decline and renewal.

STATE REGULATION AND EMPLOYMENT RIGHTS

The state plays a key role in shaping employment through regulations and employment rights. It sets the terms within which employment is legally practiced. There are important differences between civil law and common law systems. In countries with civil law systems, more emphasis is put on legislation as the primary source of law, while in common law systems, the judiciary plays a more important role, with judgements establishing legal precedents.

Broadly speaking, there are nine areas of employment law (Schregle and Jenks, 2017) as explained in Table 4.1.

Across each of these factors, state regulation can have an important impact on both the content and form of employment. The law plays an important role in employment, as Zoe Adams explains:

> the law provides the conditions in which human labour comes to function to support the process of capital accumulation, and to do so in a highly specific way. Law, as an embodiment of institutionalized power, was an integral part of the way in which land was forcefully appropriated, and most of the population deprived of access to the direct means of subsistence ... The law's role in the constitution of work generates a structural necessity for legal regulation of work, because of the power relations inherent in it generate the potential for conflict *over* work (ie its organization and remuneration) and over the relationship between work and unpaid care as well.
>
> (Adams, 2022, 3–4)

It is also worth noting that regulations and laws may only apply to what is considered legal with employment. There may be forms of employment, unpaid work, or other activities that exist outside of regulation – or that employers that choose to ignore regulations or break the law. In the UK context, there is a common law system that shapes the role of law in employment. A summary of the different laws and regulations that cover employment can be found on the UK government's gov.uk website. For employers, this includes the list presented in Table 4.2.

The table shows the range of laws and regulations that employers need to be aware of when entering into employment. The UK government also provides information for workers, which includes the list presented in Table 4.3.

The tables provide guidance for how employment law and other regulations affect employment in the UK. However, as can be seen from the tables, this is not straightforward, and it covers a wide range of aspects. In part, this is a result of the wide range of primary legislation, as well as legal judgements, that constitute employment law in the UK. For example, there are a series of Acts that affect employment:

Health and Safety at Work Act 1974. The act introduces a legal responsibility for employers to ensure a safe working environment. This covers aspects like risk assessment, training,

DOI: 10.4324/9781003279907-5

Table 4.1 Law and the Implications for Employment

Area of law	Implication for employment
Employment	Employment as a category is a relatively new phenomenon. From the end of the Second World War, policy shift from reducing unemployment to employment opportunities. This is a higher-level part of regulation, which impacts on the following parts.
Individual employment relationships	The employment relationship developed from the 'law of master and servant' with a contractual agreement for one party to be under control of another. In return for that control, the worker is paid a wage and has minimum conditions protected. From this starting point, further laws and regulations have been applied to the individual relationship.
Wages and remuneration	The law covers forms and methods of payment, including how they are determined, minimum wages, other benefits, and protections against unlawful deductions.
Conditions of work	Conditions can include aspects like the number of hours worked, break periods, holidays and so on. The law in this area started with legislation to protect children and women at work during the industrial revolution. While this began as preventions, the law has developed into guarantees for equality between genders at work. The principle of one rest day per week began as a religious practice, but has mostly developed into the regulation of five-day weeks.
Health, safety, and welfare	The law is concerned with occupational health and accident prevention, often with specific regulation for hazardous forms of work.
Social security	This can cover a range of different forms of social security from basic liability of employers to accidents at work, all the way up to comprehensive schemes that cover income, injury, sickness, unemployment, parental leave, medical care, and retirement. This is often connected to state regulation and provision of the welfare state.
Trade unions and industrial relations	The law varies widely with respect to industrial relations, including the legal status, rights, and obligations of trade unions and employers' organisations, representation at workplace and enterprise level, consultation, codetermination, collective bargaining, collective agreements, the prevention and settlement of labour disputes, and so on. In the UK and the USA in particular, there has been a trend towards the expansion of the role of law in industrial relations.
The administration of labour law	Another part of labour law is the way in which administrative authorities are organised and function, including labour departments, labour inspection services, and other enforcement bodies. This may include aspects like labour courts or tribunals, as well as bodies established to settle grievances that emerge from employment.
Special provisions for particular occupational or other groups	It is common for labour law to include provisions for specific kinds of employment or workers. These may limit legislative provisions for groups or include special provisions. For example, in agriculture, mining, transport, or commercial occupations.

Source: Adapted from Schregle and Jenks, 2017

Table 4.2 Employing People

Contracts of employment and working hours	Includes types of worker, employee rights, overtime, and changes to contracts
Dismissing staff and redundancies	Resignations, dismissals, disciplinaries, and redundancy pay
Health and safety at work	Accidents, health and safety law, and workplace conditions
Payroll	PAYE for employers, getting started, reporting and paying HMRC, expenses, and benefits
Pensions for your staff	Includes workplace pensions and Combined Pension Statements
Recruiting and hiring	Advertise a job, Disclosure and Barring (DBS) checks, right to work checks, discrimination law, and apprenticeships
Statutory leave and time off	Includes maternity and paternity leave, holiday entitlement, and sick pay
Trade unions and worker rights	Includes industrial action and recognising trade unions

Source: Adapted from gov.uk, 2022a

Table 4.3 Working, Jobs, and Pensions

Armed forces	Includes reserve forces and armed forces pensions, benefits, and financial assistance
Finding a job	Job search, Jobseekers' Allowance (JSA), job offers, right to work share codes, apprenticeships, and volunteering
Holidays, time off, sick leave, maternity and paternity leave	Includes career breaks and the holiday entitlement calculator
Redundancies, dismissals, and disciplinaries	Includes solving a workplace dispute, calculating redundancy pay, and dismissal
State Pensions	Calculating State Pension, Pension Credit, eligibility, claiming, and deferring
Workplace and personal pensions	Includes automatic enrolment, lost pensions, and planning for retirement
Your contract and working hours	Includes employment status, workers' rights, and changes to contracts
Your pay, tax, and the National Minimum Wage	Includes National Minimum Wage rates, keeping pay records, and pay rights
Your rights at work and trade unions	Includes health and safety, accidents at work, and joining a trade union

Source: Adapted from gov.uk, 2022b

and safety equipment. It established the Health and Safety Executive which enforces these duties.

Trade Union and Labour Relations (Consolidation) Act 1992. Defines trade union rights and duties, protects the rights of workers to organise into a union without discrimination or detriment, introduces a framework for collective bargaining, and protects the rights of workers to take industrial action and strike.

Employment Rights Act 1996. This act includes a range of employment rights that cover contracts, unfair dismissal, parental leave, and redundancy. It updated many previous employment regulations.

Employment Tribunals Act 1996. Established Employment Tribunals and Employment Appeals Tribunals.

National Minimum Wage Act 1998. Introduced the minimum wage and the framework for different ages and increases.

Working Time Regulations 1998. Includes right to a 20-minute paid break for each 6 hours worked, at least 24 hours uninterrupted rest each week, paid annual leave of 28 days, and limits the working week to 48 hours (with optional opt-out).

Employment Relations Act 1999. Included many employment rights, including the right of recognition for trade unions and the right for employees to be accompanied to disciplinary hearings.

Maternity and Parental Leave etc Regulations 1999. Introduced new rights for parents to take time off work.

Part-Time Workers (Prevention of Less Favourable Treatment) Regulations 2000. Introduced law to ensure comparable treatment between part-time and full-time employees.

Transfer of Undertakings (Protection of Employment) Regulations 2006. This protection employee rights during a business transfer, for example when one company is bought by another.

Equalities Act 2010. Regulates discrimination in recruitment and the workplace. Includes protected characteristics that cannot be used as a reason for making workplace decisions, including age, gender reassignment, being married or in a civil partnership, being pregnant or on maternity leave, disability, race including colour, nationality, ethic or national origin, religion or belief, sex, sexual orientation.

Agency Workers Regulations 2010. This act aims to prevent discrimination of workers employed through employment agencies.

Trade Union Act 2016. An act that amended the Trade Union and Labour Relations (Consolidation) Act 1992 to introduce limits on trade unions, including 50% turnout requirement in postal ballots for unions to take strike action.

Data Protection Act 2018. In combination with GDPR (General Data Protection Regulations) and the Data Protection Act 1998, includes the requirement that employers must gain consent for gathering, processing, and storing employees' data.

Historically, many of these rights would be enforced through collective bargaining or organising at work. However, over time there has been a change in the role of the law in the employment relationship. In the UK there has been a 'progressive juridification of the employment relationship as legal regulation has encompassed more and more aspects of the wage-work bargain' (Heery, 2010, 71).

As an example of how this has changed the employment relationship, there are two major ways this juridification is expressed. First, the process of taking industrial action. Rather than a union meeting deciding to go on strike, there are strict requirements for that action to be legally protected. First, the union members must be in a trade dispute with their employers that cannot be solved through negotiation. This means it must be a dispute between workers and their employers over issues relating to their work, rather than broader issues. This cannot involve what is called 'secondary action', taken in solidarity with other workers, for example. The union must then organise a postal ballot with an independent scrutineer. A 'Notice of Ballot' must be provided by the union to the employer with seven days' notice, identifying who will be balloted. The 'ballot paper' must have specific information relating to the dispute and type of action, as well as a clear 'yes' and 'no' option for members. The ballots need be sent by post to the address of each member, who then return these by post to the independent scrutineer. The union covers the cost of the ballot and postal charges.

The postal ballot requires a turnout of over 50% of eligible voters, with a majority in favour of strike action. In specific public services, the 'yes' vote must be above 40% of those eligible to vote overall. If these conditions are met, then the union has a valid mandate for industrial action that lasts six months. Before industrial action can take place, the union must give 14 days' notice to the employer. This must include which category of employee will be taking industrial action and whether the action will be continuous or discontinuous. If continuous, the start date must be given. If discontinuous the dates of the action must be provided. At any point during this process, the employer can apply for an injunction to stop the action from the High Court. If the union or individual members do not follow these conditions, they no longer have statutory immunity while taking industrial action. If a union refuses to comply, the employer can sue for up to £250,000 in damages. If a union does not comply with an injunction, it will be in contempt of court and can be further fined, have assets seized, or officials imprisoned. Similarly, individuals who are deprived of goods or services because of industrial action have the 'citizen's right to prevent disruption' and can apply for a legal injunction.

In addition to these requirements, there is also ACAS (the Advisory, Conciliation, and Arbitration Service) and a system of Employment Tribunals. For a worker to complain that their rights have been breached, they must go through a series of steps. First, they have to fill out an 'ET1' form and notify ACAS that they have attempted conciliation. They must then present evidence to the Employment Tribunal after which there will be a judgement. Either side may then appeal to the Employment Appeal Tribunal, then the Court of Appeal, and the Supreme Court. There are a range of other government bodies that are meant to play a role in regulation, including the Central Arbitration Committee, HM Revenue and Customs, the Equality and Human Rights Commission, the Health and Safety Executive, Low Pay Commission, and three enforcement bodies – the Gangmasters and Labour Abuse Authority, Employment Agency Standards Inspectorate, and the National Minimum Wage Team – that there has been debate about combining into a single labour market enforcement body.

Despite these extensive regulations, in the UK, as with many countries, there are major problems with the enforcement of employment law in practice. For example, the Unpaid Britain project found that £1.2 billion of wages are unpaid each year, with a further £1.5 billion in holiday pay (Clark and Herman, 2017). This is wage theft, but enforcement is often lacking. Even when a worker successfully takes a case to the Employment Tribunal and it rules in their favour, half of all awards remain unpaid. Similarly, a survey of the Employment Legal Advice Network found that 83% of organisations involved did not consider the current system to be effective in enforcing workers' rights (London Employment Legal Advice Network, 2021).

THE PUBLIC SECTOR AND THE STATE AS EMPLOYER

In addition to these factors that shape employment, the state can also be a major employer itself. This means that it is not only through regulation or intervention that the state can have an effect on employment overall, but also sets a tone for employment relationships through the kind of relationships entered into.

In 2019, statistics from the OECD showed that the proportion of employment in general government varied substantially between different countries. For example, in Norway, Sweden, and Denmark this accounts for approximately 30% of employment. Whereas in Japan it is 6% and South Korea 8%. In the UK it is 16% and the USA 15%, below the OECD average of 18%. In some countries this proportion has been falling. For example, in the UK it fell by 3% since 2007 (OECD, 2021) – although it has risen during the pandemic to 17.6% (ONS, 2022). This means that approximately one in five people are employed by the government in many countries. The

Table 4.4 Headcount of Public Sector Employment by Industry in the UK, December 2021

Construction	35,000
HM Forces	159,000
Police (including civilians)	270,000
Public administration	1,131,000
Education	1,501,000
National Health Service	1,864,000
Other health and social work	212,000
Other public sector	547,000
Total public sector	**5,721,000 (17.6%)**
Total Private sector	*26,772,000 (82.4%)*

Source: ONS, 2022

pay, conditions, and experience of working for the government shapes employment elsewhere in the economy.

As can be seen from Table 4.4, the number of people employed in the UK in the public sector is 17.6% of all those employed. Within this, a large number of people are employed in healthcare (both the NHS and other health and social work), education, and public administration. In these sectors, the state is a major employer, shaping the employment conditions for both those directly employed as well as those working within the sector.

The importance of the public sector for shaping employment comes from the different dynamics that these employees can be subject to, compared to the private sector. As Richard Rose has argued:

> Public employment is trebly important in contemporary Western societies. First of all, public employees produce many of the goods and services of the mixed-economy welfare state; their activities cover such programmes as military defence and law enforcement; nationalized enterprises selling goods in the market; and health, education and social services. Secondly, public employment is a substantial proportion of total employment; in the postwar era it has accounted for an increasing number of jobs, and grown faster than employment in the private sector. Thirdly, to millions of people public sector employment is their principal source of income, and the pay of public employees makes a major claim upon tax revenues.
>
> (Rose, 1985, xi)

This means that public sector employment is subjected to public scrutiny. It is funded through taxation (and in some cases additional charges). Due to this source of funding, there is often an expectation of accountability and transparency in the process – or at least more than in the private sector. Rather than seeking profit, there are demands to justify spending decisions made with public funding. The public sector can also be the target of political intervention, whether through interfaces with elected officials, the civil service, or the pressures of election cycles. This can be complicated by a focus on short-term results, or the intervention of non-experts in specific areas of the public sector. However, it is not the case that public sector employment can be changed at short notice – or indeed easily – by political decisions. Each new government inherits an existing public sector, governed by a complex and overlapping set of decisions and arrangements. Similarly, central government is usually only directly responsible for a small part of public sector employment (Rose, 1985, xii).

The process of managing employees can also be different in the public sector. There are three factors that influence the management approach. First, the extensive use of bureaucracy (Graeber,

2016; Weber, 1930), which can involve the use standardised rules of policies that govern employment. Second, the prevalence of professions within public sector employment. For example, teachers, nurses, doctors, civil servants, and so on. Professions like these tend to have professional norms that have developed over time, as well as specific regulations and sometimes professional or licensing bodies. Third, there is often a public service ethos involved with employment in the sector. People who work in the public sector have often chosen to do so because they believe in public service. However, in practice this can be complicated by views of the public sector as inefficient compared to other ways of organising services.

These negative views of the public sector have developed historically. In the early phase of the growth of the public sector during the establishment of the welfare state in the 1930s, this involved the introduction of a new social settlement after the Second World War. There was expansion of public services, particularly in housing, education, and health, as well as with new insurance and pension benefits. The state was positioned as a model employer, setting the terms for employment relations more widely. In terms of the HR system, this involved employment and careers that could last for a lifetime, often with regular promotion and high benefits. From the 1980s onwards, new forms of public management were introduced alongside the broader economic, political, and social changes. The rise of right-wing politics involved an emphasis on a small state, reducing spending on public services. This was introduced in practice through widespread privatisation programmes, new managerial approaches in the public sector, and competition. HR practices from the private sector were increasingly introduced, as well as performance management and performance-related pay.

These sweeping changes from the 1980s onwards are often discussed as 'neoliberalism', with the later changes from the 2010s as 'austerity' – directly referencing lower spending. Neoliberalism is an often-used, but less commonly explained, term. David Harvey argues that neoliberalism is:

> in the first instance a theory of political economic practices that propose that human well-being can best be advanced by liberating individual entrepreneurial freedoms and skills within an institutional framework characterized by strong private property rights, free markets, and free trade.
>
> (Harvey, 2007, 2)

These practices have become part of many government agendas since the 1970s. The implementation of these practices has had a far-reaching impact on employment, both within and beyond the public sector. There have been programmes of 'deregulation, privatization, and withdrawal of the state from many areas of social provision' (Harvey, 2007, 3).

The three different moments of public sector management are also closely related to three moments in which important changes took place – that are often discussed as part of neoliberalism. There was a transformative point towards the end of the 1970s and the start of the 1980s. This was a shift from the previous period of the post-Second World War settlement in the Global North. This has been discussed as a form of class compromise. While there had been an extended period of relatively high economic growth rates and low levels of unemployment, this came to an end. During this prior period, a section of workers – predominantly white men – had worked with the expectation of continuous and relatively secure employment. This went alongside expectations of access to housing and mass-produced commodities, including things like cars, televisions, washing machines, fridges, and so on. There was also an important role for the state, providing education, healthcare, social security, pensions, and so on. However, this compromise did not last.

In the late 1970s, the global economy entered into a structural crisis. There were falling profits and a severe energy crisis. This resulted in an economic phenomenon known as stagflation in which inflation and unemployment increased while growth declined. The response to this crisis was the development and implementation of a 'new social order' that has become known as neoliberalism (Duménil and Lévy, 2005, 9). This new social order did not happen by accident. It was developed and tested before it became implemented more widely. The first instance of experimentation can be found in the economic policies implemented after the 1973 military coup in Chile. Economists who were trained in the USA (known as the 'Chicago Boys') returned to Chile, using the US-backed coup against the democratically elected socialist government of Salvador Allende as an opportunity to radically reshape the Chilean economy. Naomi Klein has called this approach the 'shock doctrine', using a crisis as a moment of opportunity to implement things that would not have otherwise been possible (Klein, 2008). Following Chile, neoliberal reforms were taken up by the governments of Margaret Thatcher in Britain and Ronald Reagan in the USA. In terms of employment, this meant the 'labour market was to be "deregulated" and labour made more "flexible"', however this would be on the employers', not the workers' terms (Munke, 2005, 62). An important part of this was undermining workers' power and trade union organisation. It was therefore a project that aimed to restore 'management's "right to manage" … in all its splendour' making sure that the 'market would not be allowed to suffer from "political" constraints' (Munke, 2005, 62). In the 1990s neoliberal policies were consolidated. This can be understood as a moment in which there was 'a "roll out" of new policies rather than just a "roll back" of the state' (Munke, 2005, 63). Further changes to employment were introduced, as well as reforms to welfare, urban regeneration, and migration.

From the 2010s onwards, there were further changes to the public sector that have an important implication for employment. There were substantial cuts to public spending and wage freezes for many public sector workers. This can be seen as a 'deprivileging' of the public sector workforce (Bach, 2016). The British government bailed out the financial crisis, nationalising banks and paying out huge amounts of money. At the same time as the state extended in this way, it also further retreated from the public sector, introducing more private companies into the provision of previously public sector functions (Lodge and Hood, 2012). The aggressive 'privatisation' introduced with neoliberalism forms 'the cutting edge of accumulation by dispossession', as discussed earlier in chapter 2 (Harvey, 2003, 157). The process involves undermining and reducing the welfare state in the 1980s and the response to the 2008 financial crisis: austerity programmes that involved reducing workers' wages and conditions, limiting public spending, and further privatisation of public services.

POST-INDUSTRIAL EMPLOYMENT

The social, economic, and political factors discussed above have brought significant changes to employment. It is also important to understand that the labour process has also changed significantly, both over the longer historical scope outlined in chapter 1, as well as through the more recent neoliberal period. Technology has long played a role in the labour process, from early tools and machineries, all the way up to the most complex modern digital infrastructures.

Technology is applied to the labour process to achieve two objectives, as discussed in chapter 1. First, it increases productivity. This involves what Marx called the increase in 'relative surplus value', as technology speeds up tasks or allows workers to get more done in the same amount of time (Marx, 1867, 643). Second, technology is also used to increase control in the workplace. For example, Marx also argued that 'it would be possible to write a whole history of the inventions made since 1830 for the sole purpose of providing capital with weapons against working-class revolt' (Marx, 1867, 563). This is something that is often missed in discussions of technology. Instead of understanding the ways in which it is developed from, and then used within, existing social relations, technologies are sometimes presented as linear steps in a development. One technology follows from the last, and each is a better iteration. Braverman argues that:

> machinery offers to management the opportunity to do by wholly mechanical means that which it had previously attempted to do by organizational and disciplinary means The fact that machines

may be paced and controlled according to centralized decisions, and that these controls may thus be in the hands of management, removed from the site of production to the office – these technical possibilities are of just as great interest to management as the fact that the machine multiplies the productivity of labor.

(Braverman, 1998, 134)

Thus, technological change is part of a process of transforming employment, both to be more productive, as well as offering new possibilities of control.

These changes can be seen throughout manufacturing and other forms of industrial work that have been subject to huge technological change. Modern factories require far less workers and have a productivity that is often many times greater. However, these changes can also be seen in the emergence of new kinds of service work like call centres (Woodcock, 2017) and platform work (Woodcock, 2022).

Today, many more people in Britain work in what is broadly called the 'service sector', often in forms of employment that have been enabled or deeply shaped by new technology. Employment in services differs from other forms like manufacturing, because it involves the commodification of a process rather the commodification of an output (Gronroos, 1990). This can be hairdressing, hospitality, finance, education, healthcare, or entertainment. There are a wide range of services that are bought and sold in contemporary society, including many that rely upon other forms of production. The exact definition of services can be less clear than sectors like manufacturing, because of the wide diversity of activities involved. However, there are some key characteristics of services that can help to make sense of this as outlined in Table 4.5.

These characteristics mean that the worker becomes part of the experience of the customer, introducing new pressures and demands compared to other forms of employment. As the worker can act as a representative of the company, the job role can expand to include aspects of marketing. Most commonly, this is seen with upselling in service encounters. Whether this is the call centre worker attempting to sell another service over the phone, the retail worker offering alternative products, or the waiter suggesting dessert.

The application of technology to services has changed the operation of the work in two key ways. First, technologies have provided a way to convert high-contact services into lower-contact services that are mediated by technology. For example, much of banking services have moved away from the high street with the rise of internet banking. While this reduces employment needed in the roles, the remaining in-person forms have become more complex. For example, bank workers who have to deal with a wider range of issues and more complex financial services. Second, technology leads to the standardisation and simplification of many service jobs. For example, call centre technologies provide a way to greatly increase the number of mediated service encounters that workers can undertake, but it can also lead to high levels of stress and turnover, as well as negative experiences for customers (Woodcock, 2017).

These aspects of service employment present many challenges for effective management. It can be hard to set goals or measure performance, which makes management of service workers much harder. There may also be tensions between quantitative and qualitative targets as these can differ widely in services. Worker satisfaction and customer satisfaction can become connected in service work, in a way that did not exist in manufacturing (Heskett et al., 1997). This has become part of 'new service management' which focuses on the idea of a 'satisfaction mirror' that links workers and customers. Satisfied workers provide a higher quality of customer service, leading to higher customer satisfaction. Similarly, a failure to satisfy customers can be a source of frustration for workers.

This has a range of implications for managers. First, that managers need to try to recruit and select workers that have the desired personality traits and attitudes for service employment, as many of these can be difficult to train for. Second, that there need to be support systems in

Table 4.5 Characteristics of Service Work

Characteristic	Explanation
Intangibility	Services are not tangible, meaning they are physically immaterial and mentally intangible. This means it can be difficult to measure. Not only might the service have little in terms of material output (like an educational course), but it may be difficult to provide a clear example of exactly what constitutes quality or compare different options. For managers, this makes it comparatively difficult to measure worker performance or productivity.
Variability	Services vary both in terms of workers' performance and customers requirement. For example, there are many different kinds of haircuts, both in terms of what customers want, as well as the options offered by hairdressers. There is much more variability compared to the manufacturing of scissors used to cut hair. It is therefore much harder to standardise the delivery of services, as well as not being what customers might want.
Perishability of output	Unlike manufacturing, there is no inventory of output. Put simply, services cannot be placed on a shelf if the customer is not ready for it. This means that when demand is low, any unused capacity is wasted. When demand is high, there is no buffer of inventory that can be drawn upon. The overall service quality might deteriorate as attempts are made to meet demand. For managers, this means that trying to forecast demand it important.
Simultaneity of consumption and production	Related to the above, consumption and production of services often happens at the same time. When this does happen, the service encounter requires the presence of the customer (although this can be mediated in different ways) who can become a co-producer of the service. Some services also involve customer to customer, as well as worker to customer relationships.

Source: Batt, 2009

place for service workers, as well as some discretion for those providing the service, and effective teamwork with back office workers. Third, that measurement systems, as well as rewards, should be based on customer service measures, rather than measures driven by the organisation. Fourth, that the development of a customer service culture can also act as a form of control over workers (Korczynski, 2002).

There have been criticisms of this approach as it risks conflating the different forms of service work. For example, some services are provided as a mass market offering, while others are much more specialised and personalised. There have also been criticisms about the creation of a large number of low wage service work that do not offer training or career paths. This has been captured in the term 'McDonaldisation' which stretches far beyond only the fast food chain (Ritzer, 1993). There are also many challenges that stem from the introduction of emotion into the labour process, which will be discussed in the next section.

One solution to these challenges has been the emergence of contingent HRM strategies in service employment. These are related to the differences in customer segmentation between the high value added (including forms of professional services, healthcare, and so on) and the low value added (retail and fast food). These differences can be seen in Table 4.6.

Table 4.6 Contingent HRM Strategies

Service Market Type	Knowledge content of service	Typical work design	Competitive dynamics in the sector	Predictions for HR strategy in firms
Type 1 Mass-service markets (eg petrol stations, fast food, supermarkets)	Low, Key managers or franschisees have critical knowledge, but general labour uses limited, mostly generic 'know-how'	Low discretion. May be highly 'Taylorised' in international franchises or major chains; otherwise unrationalised, low-skill work	Cost-based except to the extent limited by unions and state regulation; substitution of labour for technology and self-service; some branding strategies possible	Firms typically fit HR strategy to their cost-driven competitive strategies through paying only the market-clearing wage and complying minimally with labour laws; very limited prospects for HR advantage, except where premium brands can be created and sustained
Type 2 A mix of mass market and higher value-added segments (eg elder care, hotels, call centres)	Low-to-moderate knowledge levels; mix of skill level needed in the workforce	Traditionally low-to-moderate discretion, but potential for job enrichment and HPWSs	Mix of cost and quality-based competition; greater profit opportunities for firms that identify higher value-added segments	In mass markets, HR strategies are Type 1, but possibilities exist for HR advantage in higher value-added segments; potential problems with imitability and appropriability
Type 3 Very significantly, if not totally, differentiated markets (eg high-level professional services)	High knowledge intensity	High discretion – the natural home of HPWSs	Expertise and quality-based competition, but with some anchors on relative pricing; some services may be routinised and migrate back to Type 2 competition	Extensive opportunities for HR advantage in expertise-driven niches; potential problems with imitability and appropriability; use of lower cost HR strategies where expertise is routinised

Source: Boxall, 2003, 13

As can be seen from the table, mass market services aim to substitute workers for technology where possible – or encourage customer self-service. For example, the use of self-service checkouts in supermarkets or the growth of online banking. This leads to lower paid jobs in which the labour process is highly scripted. On the other hand, high value added services involve much higher discretion in the labour process and workers are paid more. There is also more opportunity for management to make investments in HR techniques.

EMOTIONAL LABOUR

The shift from industrial to service work has involved a change in the kind of activities involved in this form of employment. One of the important aspects of service work is that it often involves creating an experience for a customer. For example, when a customer buys a drink in a coffee shop, they are paying for more than just ground beans and hot water. There is an interaction between the customer and the employee which takes place in a curated environment. In some cases, this experience is also measured and rewarded by the customer in the form of a variable percentage tip.

Although it does not always take place in the context of tipping, more employment now involves the use of emotions. Arlie Hochschild argued that 'emotional labour' was an important part of service work (Hochschild, 1983). As part of her research, she identified the emotional labour of flight attendants. Airplanes are particular kind of service workplace. Customers cannot leave the airplane during the journey and flight attendants must try and put them at ease, both through the use of their emotions and with food and drink. Hochschild defined emotional labour as 'the management of feeling to create a publicly observable facial and bodily display' (Hochschild, 1983, 7). In the case of flight attendants, anyone who has travelled by airplane (or seen representations of this on TV or film) can recognise this process. Flight attendants moving up and down the cabin with trolleys, providing refreshments, and checking in on the passengers. Each customer is smiled at – with the worker having to maintain the smile and demeanour throughout even long-haul flights.

Emotions have always played a part in work. During the industrial revolution there were a substantial number of domestic servants, using their emotions throughout the labour process. However, this kind of emotional labour has historically been devalued and considered as unskilled, particularly in relation to traditionally masculine roles. As Dalla Costa and James have argued, 'where women are concerned, their labour appears to be a personal service outside of capital' (Dalla Costa and James, 1971, 10). Thus, when it is brought into paid work, it is often not considered as something that needs to be paid as a skill. The gendering of work (and indeed in the divisions over what is considered to be work) has involved the devaluation of the work and skills historically associated with women. In the case of care and domestic work they can be unpaid or often not considered to be real forms of work. In many kinds of gendered work, 'women do not gain and retain jobs becau se of the particular occupational resources they possess … but rather they are employed as "women" with an assumed responsiveness' (Adkins and Lury, 1999, 605).

As discussed in the section before with service work, the labour process of flight attendants is quite different to that of a factory worker. In the factory, the output can be clearly measured. However, for the flight attendant, the 'emotional style of offering the service is part of the service itself'. As Hochschild continues:

> This labor requires one to induce or suppress feeling in order to sustain the outward countenance that produces the proper state of mind in others – in this case, the sense of being cared for in a convivial and safe place. This kind of labor calls for a coordination of mind and feeling, and it sometimes draws on a source of self that we honor as deep and integral to our individuality.
>
> (Hochschild, 1983, 7)

We can see a moment of this in many service encounters: the barista in a coffee shop greeting us, the call centre worker responding to our questions, the supermarket cashier wishing us a good day, or the bar worker listening to the troubles of a drinker. This emotional labour is central to customer service roles. It is an integral part of how products and services are marketed, sold, and consumed. This emotional component of work has become widespread across many kinds of low-paid employment. However, 'even a child ... knows that the smile and "have a great day" from a customer-service-worker is fundamentally creepy' (Cederström and Fleming, 2012, 7). It is a human emotion repurposed in order to try and sell things.

This is because emotional labour introduces new demands at work. In the study of call centre workers, Hochschild referred to this as the 'pinch', or the conflict between the feelings of the worker and what company demands from them (Hochschild, 1983, xi). The 'creepiness' of this is that we know a worker in customer services has to say 'have a great day', regardless of how their own is going. This process can introduce a form of emotional dissonance, leading to increased stress and exhaustion. For example, in call centres, this can create 'feelings of guilt and stress callers experience as they try to convince customers to buy insurance while maintaining a positive and enthusiastic demeanour' (Woodcock, 2017, 53). Other studies have found that 'emotional dissonance may ultimately lead to lowered self-esteem, depression, cynicism, and alienation from work' (Lewig and Dollard, 2003, 368).

Given the range of work in which these demands now exist, the concept of emotional labour has been developed further into the idea of 'affective labour'. Beyond just involving emotions, affective labour 'refers equally to body and mind' and the activity 'produces or manipulates affects' (Hardt and Negri, 2004, 108). The affective labour process attempts to produce 'intangible feelings of ease, excitement, or passion' (Hardt and Negri, 2001, 293). This can spread out beyond just customer service interactions, involving a:

> series of activities that are not normally recognized as 'work' – in other words, the kinds of activities involved in defining and fixing cultural and artistic standards, fashions, tastes, consumer norms, and, more strategically, public opinion.
>
> (Lazzarato, 1996, 133)

Call centres provide an often precarious and low-paid example of emotional and affective labour. The demand from managers for workers to 'smile down the phone' is similar to the 'outward countenance' of flight attendants, albeit mediated through computers and phones (Taylor and Bain, 1999, 103). There are particular pressures for performing this kind of labour. Research highlights how 'working in a call centre tends to include a well-established mix of low wages, high stress, precarious employment, rigid management, draining emotional labour and pervasive electronic surveillance' (Brophy, 2010, 471). The labour process also often involve hostility from customers, meaning there is also the anger of others to be managed in the process (Deery et al., 2002). For workers calling across national borders, this can also mean demands for 'authenticity' to be performed, including taking on different names and learning local facts to hide the international connection (Mirchandani, 2012). In my own research I found that:

> The affective package that workers are required to perform during the labour process is demanding. The experience was exhausting and emotionally draining. From my own experience of working eight-hour afternoon/evening shifts – unfortunately also complemented with a morning of reading and writing about call centres – the labour process was exhausting. In particular it made social phone calls something to avoid, as I became unable to break out of the routinised pattern of sales calls; in-person conversations became difficult too. Arriving home by about 10pm, my food preparation fell into a pattern of baked beans on toast, followed by slouching on the sofa watching television.
>
> (Woodcock, 2017, 53–54)

However, these demands and pressures are not limited to call centres. Across many forms of employment, the use of 'creativity' and 'self-expression' have become necessary parts of the labour process, leading to 'affective, as well as productive demands on workers' (Fisher, 2009, 40).

PRECARIOUS WORK

Precarious work, or an unstable or insecure employment relationship, has become a popular topic in academic research. Precariousness is often discussed as if it were a break from a form of stable employment, often considered in terms of the 'standard employment relationship' discussed in chapter 1. There can be some difficulty in pinning down definitions of precarious work. The ILO uses the following definition:

> In the most general sense, precarious work is a means for employers to shift risks and responsibil-ities on to workers. It is work performed in the formal and informal economy and is characterized by variable levels and degrees of objective (legal status) and subjective (feeling) characteristics of uncertainty and insecurity. Although a precarious job can have many faces, it is usually defined by uncertainty as to the duration of employment, multiple possible employers or a disguised or ambiguous employment relationship, a lack of access to social protection and benefits usually associated with employment, low pay, and substantial legal and practical obstacles to joining a trade union and bargaining collectively.
>
> (International Labour Organization, 2011, 5)

On the other hand, Pierre Bourdieu, defined '*précarité*' as a:

> new mode of domination in public life ... based on the creation of generalized and permanent state of insecurity aimed at forcing workers into submission, into the acceptance of exploitation. To characterize this mode of domination ... a speaker here proposed the very expressive concept of flexploitation. The word evokes the rational management of insecurity ... what is presented as an economic system ... is in reality a political system which can only be set up with the active or passive complicity of the official political powers.
>
> (Bourdieu, 1998, 95–99)

These are two related, but different, definitions. The first speaks to the changes in conditions in the employment relationship, while the second makes a broader claim about the reasons for these changes and their societal effect.

In order to make sense of these definitions, it is important to dig into two parts mentioned in the ILO definition. The first is the 'objective' change in terms and conditions away from stable and predictable employment. Undoubtedly, in many occupations and sectors, employment is more precarious than it used to be. Considered against the longer historical trends, this could be seen as a return to conditions that existed before, albeit returning in a new way. The second, and harder to pin down, is the 'subjective' experience of precarity.

The feeling of precarity in employment is something that many people can relate to today. Many jobs feel harder to get, as well as harder to keep hold of. Alongside this, preparation for employment, whether through education (and the high levels of student debt that many have to take on in the process) or undertaking internships (Perlin, 2012), has increased the pressure. Forms of precarious work may involve a lower 'actual amount of time spent doing paid work', but they also involve workers having to 'be continually available for such work' (Mitropoulos, 2005, 13).

The kinds of employment matter for how this precarity is experienced. For example, Kidd McKarthy introduces the distinction of 'BrainWorkers', 'who are hired not for their gen-eral labour but for specialised skills or their creativity', while 'ChainWorkers' are employed in minimum wage jobs and are like 'automatons and the only thing they have to sell is their labour' (McKarthy, 2005, 57). For example, compare the freelance software developer who works contract to contract with the fast food worker who does not know what shifts they will work the following week. Both are experiencing precarity and instability in their employment, however the former has many advantages over the latter. Their labour-power can attract a higher payment, there is perhaps the opportunity to bargain, and the demand for their skills offers more opportunities. Low-paid workers, on the other hand, have much less of a buffer to deal with the effects of precarity. It is important to consider these differences because there is an increasing polarisation between jobs (Kaplanis, 2007) and an increasing number of those at the bottom that could be considered 'lousy jobs' (Goos and Manning, 2007).

Workers enter into precarious employment relationships with different resources to cope with the conditions. For example, migrant workers are often particularly at risk from precarity. The employment of migrant workers may be tied to specific visa requirements – sometimes tying them to specific employers – or they may work with irregular status. This puts additional pressure on the stability of their relationships, not only is employment at risk, but also residency and the right to remain in a country (Ryan, 2005). Women workers are already more likely to be working in 'nonstandard' jobs that are casualised or temporary (Fredman, 2003). They may have to balance precarious work with other pressures, for example, care or family responsibilities that fall disproportionately on women workers. In these cases, precarity intersects with other vulnerabilities that workers may face, particularly in low-paid 'nonstandard' jobs that are not covered by any of the 'three regulatory regimes—collective bargaining, employment protection rights, and the national insurance system' (Fredman, 2003, 308). Indeed, where 'low pay and non-unionisation' combine, this vulnerability is likely to be sharpest (Pollert and Charlwood, 2009, 344).

For some in the literature the growth of low-paid precarious employment is an important phenomenon. Guy Standing argued that the difference in experience of employment for precarious workers is so pronounced that it is creating a new class of people: the precariat (Standing, 2011). However, at the same time, others in the literature have argued that the objective changes are either not as significant or that job tenure is actually increasing (Doogan, 2009). This is where the importance of the 'subjective' feeling of precariousness matters. This also needs to be connected to the broader trends and context within which people feel more precarious (even if they are not objectively so). As noted earlier in the chapter, the preceding context for contemporary employment is often discussed in terms of neoliberalism. A key part of neoliberal reforms has been the:

> extensive deregulation of labour-rights, eliminated on a daily basis in all corners of the world that have industrial production and services; increase in the fragmentation of the working class, precarisation and subcontracting of the human force that labours; and destruction of class-unionism and its transformation into docile unionism, based on *partnership.*
>
> (Antunes, 2013)

There has therefore been a deliberately attempt to increase the precarity of many forms of employment, felt particularly in low-paid work that lacks trade union protection. This helps to explain why there is a 'broad public perception of the end of jobs for life and the decline of stable employment' that operates alongside 'the rise in long-term employment' (Doogan, 2009, 91). There is a wider context in which 'social, economic, and political forces have aligned to make work more precarious' (Kalleberg, 2009, 2). This involves five factors. The first is that there has been a 'decline in attachment to employers', meaning many people expect to hold different jobs over a career and are more willing to change jobs; second, there is an 'increase in long-term unemployment', with more people looking for work; third a 'growth in perceived job insecurity'; fourth, there has been 'a growth of non-standard work arrangements and contingent work';

and fifth, there has been an 'increase in risk-shifting from employers to employees' (Kalleberg, 2009, 6–8).

In particular, the subjective feeling here is particularly important. Whether or not work is actually becoming more precarious, if people feel that their work has become precarious, then it has a real effect (Seymour 2012, quoted in Woodcock, 2017, 136). Workers may accept worse conditions if they fear that they may not get a job or lose an existing one. The fear of finding new work can keep people in jobs that they do not want to stay. Precariousness also reduces the confidence of workers to try and change their employment – to raise their 'voice' as Human Resource Management would put it.

PLATFORMS AND THE GIG ECONOMY

In terms of employment, the gig economy and platform work are often touted as driving major changes in employment. The two terms are related, but also have important differences. The gig economy involves precarious work, with many similarities in terms of the previous section of the chapter. The term comes from 'gig', referring to the short-term arrangement for musicians to play at a venue. There is likely no guarantee of anything like regular work, although they may be invited back if the performance is really well received (Woodcock and Graham, 2019, 3). There have been gigs of one kind or another for a very long time in employment. Much employment during the industrial revolution was precarious. For example, dockers had long been employed precariously, getting work when there is demand.

The gig economy is often combined with the rise of platforms. This marks it out as a more recent phenomenon, becoming more popular in the academic literature in the last decade (Kessler, 2018). Platforms are an increasingly important part of the economy, affecting not only working relationships (Vallas and Schor, 2020), but also culture (Poell et al., 2022), changing the relationship of consumption of television and music (for example, Netflix), music (Spotify), and video games (Steam). In terms of work platforms, these provide 'tools to bring together the supply of, and demand for, labour' (Graham and Woodcock, 2018, 242). This involves smart-phone applications and digital infrastructures, as well as artificial intelligence and algorithms for managing the work (Aloisi and De Stefano, 2022; Woodcock, 2020). Nick Srnicek argues that:

> Platforms, in sum, are a new type of firm; they are characterized by providing the infrastructure to intermediate between different user groups, by displaying monopoly tendencies driven by network effects, by employing cross-subsidization to draw in different user groups, and by having designed a core architecture that governs the interaction possibilities.
>
> (Srnicek, 2017, 48)

An important part of this model has involved platforms engaging workers as independent or self-employed contractors. However, there has been an extensive debate, both in the academic literature as well as in the courts, on this question of employment classification. Legal scholars have argued that platforms are employers (De Stefano, 2019; Aloisi, 2016), as well as challenged the 'bogus self-employment' used by platforms and legally contested them (Kirk, 2020).

Broadly speaking, there are two kinds of platform work. The first is what has been termed 'geographically tethered work' (Woodcock and Graham, 2019). This is work that needs to be completed in a particular place. For example, being transported as a passenger, having takeaway food delivered, or a house cleaned. All these kinds of work have existed before platforms, but companies like Uber, Lyft, Deliveroo, Meituan, Helpling, and Housekeep have reconfigured the relationship between company, worker, and customer. These activities are now being organised through smartphone apps and over the internet. Although the work itself still happens in a similar way. Across many cities and towns, the respective uniforms and colours of delivery workers have become a very common sight. The second kind is 'cloudwork' (Woodcock and Graham, 2019). This is work that can happen regardless of the place, so long as the worker has access to a computer and internet connection. Within this kind of work, workers can complete very short tasks (or microwork) on platforms like Amazon's Mechanical Turk (Sherry, 2020; Irani and Silberman, 2013), or engage in longer freelance type tasks on platforms like Freelancer or UpWork.

It should come as no surprise that technology – and particularly artificial intelligence and algorithms – have become an important focus in understanding this work. However, Table 4.7

Table 4.7 Where Did the Gig Economy Come From?

Precondition	Factor	Explanation
Platform infrastructure	Technology	This includes the technologies necessary to mediate work digitally. For some companies, this requires the capacity to organise many transactions and simultaneously direct the work. Platforms go beyond simply being a marketplace that connect consumers and workers, instead they often involve complex calculations, surveillance, and attempts at control.
Digital legibility of work	Technology	This refers to whether the work can be measured in a way that allows it to become platformised. It should come as no surprise that transportation platforms have been successful so far. They involve discrete tasks with a clear start and end, plotted with GPS coordinates. Some forms of work would be much harder to reorganise with a platform.
Mass connectivity and cheap technology	Technology, Social	The widespread availability of smartphones and relatively cheap data connections has facilitated the growth of platform work. Over half of the world population now have access to the internet. Without this, it would be much harder to use platforms as access to them (either for workers or consumers) would carry a much higher cost.
Consumer attitudes and preferences	Social	Platforms have built upon previous behaviours of consumers, as well as encouraging others. For example, taxi transportation and food delivery existed before platforms, and consumers were used to access services in this way, albeit by phone call. There are other services that people use that they may be more hesitant to access through a platform.
Gendered and racialised relationships of work	Social	Platform work has followed existing patterns of gender and racial oppression, as well as deepening them in some cases. In particular, racialised groups (and often migrants) have been recruited into low-paid and precarious arrangements with platforms.
Desire for flexibility for/ from workers	Social, Political Economy	There has been a desire for flexibility that comes both from the platform and workers. Both sides are searching for more flexible arrangements, whether to free workers from stricter employment schedules, or for employers to only pay for workers when there is demand.

Table 4.7 (Cont.)

Precondition	Factor	Explanation
State regulation	Political Economy	State regulation has both facilitated and constrained the growth of platform work. Building upon the previous decades of neoliberalism, platforms have been able to intervene into regulatory debates, particularly in favour of self-employment classification.
Worker power	Political Economy	Existing worker power has shaped the conditions of platform work when it is introduced. In some cases workers have retain elements of benefits from beforehand, while in other cases new workers' movements are trying to reshape platform work.
Globalization and outsourcing	Political Economy, Technology	Platform work is a development of the wider processes of both outsourcing and globalisation. This involves the shifting international divisions of labour (discussed in chapter 2), as well as the continuing search for cheaper labour.

Source: (Woodcock and Graham, 2019, 20)

identifies nine different preconditions that have shaped the gig economy, including a range of factors that come from both technologies, social dynamics, and the political economy.

As can be seen from the table, there are a wide range of factors that have shaped the gig economy and platform work today. While technology has undoubtedly played a role, there is much more happening with this new phenomenon. Much of the academic debate has, however, focused on the role of technology. In particular, there has been much written on the topic of algorithmic management (Duggan et al., 2020; Rosenblat, 2018; Rosenblat and Stark, 2016; Lee et al., 2015). Arguments have emerged in the literature about the importance of data generated from the labour process (Doorn and Badger, 2020), or investigating the hidden work behind algorithms (Gray and Suri, 2019).

Perhaps one of the most interesting aspects of platform capitalism is that it has sparked a new wave of worker organising (Woodcock, 2021; Joyce et al., 2020). There has been a renewed interest in worker agency and the possibilities of trade unions to represent these workers. Part of this literature has taken a renewed interest in the labour process (Englert et al., 2020; Tassinari and Maccarrone, 2020) and undertaken ethnographic research (Cant, 2019) or co-research methods with workers (Cant and Mogno, 2020; Cant, 2018c, 2018b, 2018a; Mogno, 2018; Waters and Woodcock, 2017). Much of this research explores the strikes and protests of platform workers. There remain big questions about the implications of these actions and whether they will translate into new and sustainable forms of trade unionism.

TRADE UNION DECLINE AND RENEWAL

The final theme that this chapter discusses is trade unionism. As discussed in chapter 1, the struggles over employment, many of which involved trade unions, is an important part of the history of employment. These have reshaped employment in both small and profound ways. However, trade unions have never been a static form of organisation, instead both trying to shape and in turn being shaped by employment.

Following the 1970s, the trade union movement has been in secular decline. Membership has fallen and the sectors covered by collective agreements or bargaining continue to decline. The end of the 1970s is often taken as a turning point for trade unionism. One argument that is often put forward is that the decline in manufacturing employment (within which unions were strong) explains the decline of unions today. The 'decreased share of employment in manufacturing undoubtedly hurt unions' (Freeman and Pelletier, 1990, 3), however this change does not explain the overall trends. At the same time as employment in manufacturing was falling, there was a rise in service employment. From the 1970s onwards, there was growth in white collar trade unionism, including with women and part-time workers (Price and Bain, 1983, 5). Instead, Freeman and Pelletier argue that the reason for the most significant change in union membership was 'the legal environment for industrial relations, as reflected in laws regulating union and management behavior in the area of union recognition and membership' (Freeman and Pelletier, 1990, 6). It was therefore not a change in economic circumstances, per se, but a deliberate intervention from the state and managers to reduce the power and membership of trade unions. Union membership is not only about workers' choices to join – or not – but instead about three sets of behaviours: first, workers' choices about participating in unions; second, the tactical and strategic choices of unions; and third, the responses from managers and employers (Freeman and Pelletier, 1990, 7).

What is interesting about this is it cuts against a common argument that unions are 'outdated' or a 'thing of the past'. The neoliberal reorganisation of the economy was, in part, about reasserting 'management's "right to manage" ... in all its splendour', forcing through changes to ensure that the 'market would not be allowed to suffer from "political" constraints' (Munke, 2005, 62). Unions were therefore deliberately curtailed. In effect, they were made to be a thing of the past in many sectors, while in others they were actively prevented from starting. Indeed, quantitative analysis indicates that a key part in the decline of union recognition, density, and coverage is the failure of unions to organise in workplaces that were established after the 1980s (Machin, 2000, 631). It is therefore not so much that unions are declining across the economy (although the statistics show that is happening too), but that there is an increasing 'proportion of new union-free workplaces where unions are unable to even get a toe in the door, are trends that are unlikely to be reversed easily' (Machin, 2000, 642). Instead of unions, many of these workplaces have introduced Human Resource departments, which play a very different role. While Human Resource practices have often been touted as an alternative to unions, there is no difference in the rate of union decline in workplaces that adopt HR practices compared to those that have not (Machin and Wood, 2005).

From the 1980s onwards, the British industrial relations system (referring to the relationship between the state, employers, and trade unions), 'underwent decollectivization on a massive scale in a relatively short period of time' (Baccaro and Howell, 2017, 51). While the state had previously been concerned with industrial relations and supporting collective bargaining, this effectively ended. For the Conservative government, this went alongside privatising previously nationalised industries. As discussed in other chapters, the turning point for this was the defeat of the miners' strike. Trade unions were subjected to further legal restrictions and regulations. While legislation may have made it more difficult for trade unions, it also supported the 'slow build-up in management confidence to resist unionization' (Dunn and Metcalf, 1994, 22), meaning workplaces became increasingly hostile for trade unions.

There is debate in the academic literature about what this backdrop of changes means for workers and trade unions today. This has involved research that takes a longer perspective and introduced different forms of power that workers have (Silver, 2003), others have debated the form and model of unions, including a classic distinction between 'partnership' and 'organising' unions (Heery, 2002). There are different approaches to understanding conflict at work, including those who have tried to understand worker mobilisation (Kelly, 1998), alternative forms of worker organisation (Ness, 2014), or argue that we need to return to conflict in the labour process (Atzeni, 2009; 2021). Another area of debate is on the possibilities of union revitalisation (Phelan, 2007), which often discusses the 'turn' to organising (Ibsen and Tapia, 2017). This means returning to unions that are trying to 'organise' workers, which may appear to be the main purpose for unions, but has increasingly given way to services members' interests and other activities. Simms and Holgate have warned that it is important to work out what the organising is for, rather than just doing it (Simms and Holgate, 2010). Others in the literature have suggested that 'union renewal' is more useful, involving a much more thorough change in unions, rather than just minor changes to the organisation (Murray, 2017).

Recently, these debates have become more popular and practitioner focused. There have been a series of books on organising and trade unions (Allinson, 2022; Holgate, 2021; McAlevey, 2016). More importantly for the possibilities of renewal of unions, there have also been a wave of new unions and workers' struggles. There have been strikes of platform workers, as noted earlier in this chapter. In the USA there have been successful union votes at Amazon and Starbucks, signalling the beginnings of unions in previously unorganised sectors. In the UK, strikes have returned in 2022 to levels not seen in the previous 30 years. There have been strikes in education, transportation, postal services, and more.

REFERENCES

Adams, Z. (2022) *The legal concept of work*, Oxford, Oxford University Press.

Adkins, L. and Lury, C. (1999) 'The Labour of Identity: Performing Identities, Performing Economies', *Economy and Society*, vol. 28, no. 4, pp. 598–614.

Allinson, I. (2022) *Workers Can Win: A Guide to Organising at Work*, London, Pluto Press.

Aloisi, A. (2016) 'Commoditized workers: Case study research on labor law issues arising from a set of "on-demand/gig economy" platforms', *Comparative Labor Law and Policy Journal*, vol. 37, no. 3, pp. 620–653.

Aloisi, A. and De Stefano, V. (2022) *Your boss is an algorithm: artificial intelligence, platform work and labour*, Gordonsville, Hart Publishing, an imprint of Bloomsbury Publishing.

Antunes, R. (2013) *The Meanings of Work: Essays on the Affirmation and Negation of Work*, Chicago, IL, Haymarket Books.

Atzeni, M. (2009) 'Searching for injustice and finding solidarity? A contribution to the mobilisation theory debate', *Industrial Relations Journal*, vol. 40, no. 1, pp. 5–16.

Atzeni, M. (2021) 'Workers' organizations and the fetishism of the trade union form: toward new pathways for research on the labour movement?', *Globalizations*.

Baccaro, L. and Howell, C. (2017) *Trajectories of neoliberal transformation: European industrial relations since the 1970s*, Cambridge, Cambridge University Press [Online]. DOI: 10.1017/9781139088381.

Bach, S. (2016) 'Deprivileging the public sector workforce: Austerity, fragmentation and service withdrawal in Britain', *The Economic and Labour Relations Review*, vol. 27, no. 1, pp. 11–28 [Online]. DOI: 10.1177/1035304615627950.

Batt, R. (2009) 'Service Strategies: Marketing, Operations, and Human Resource Practices', in Boxall, P., Purcell, J. and Wright, P.M. (eds), *The Oxford Handbook of Human Resource Management*, 1st edn, Oxford University Press, pp. 428–449 [Online]. DOI: 10.1093/oxfordhb/9780199547029.003.0021 (Accessed 31 October 2022).

Bourdieu, P. (1998) *Contre Feux*, Paris, Raisons d'agir.

Boxall, P. (2003) 'HR strategy and competitive advantage in the service sector', *Human Resource Management Journal*, vol. 13, no. 3, pp. 5–20 [Online]. DOI: 10.1111/j.1748-8583.2003.tb00095.x.

Braverman, H. (1998) *Labor and Monopoly Capital: The Degradation of Work in the Twentieth Century*, New York, Monthly Review Press.

Brophy, E. (2010) 'The Subterranean Stream: Communicative Capitalism and Call Centre Labour', *Ephemera*, vol. 10, no. 3/4, pp. 470–483.

Cant, C. (2018a) 'The Wave of Worker Resistance in European Food Platforms 2016-17', *Notes from Below* [Online]. Available at https://notesfrombelow.org/article/european-food-platform-str ike-wave.

Cant, C. (2018b) 'More rider, more radical, more... break: An interview with French riders', *Notes from Below* [Online]. Available at https://notesfrombelow.org/article/more-rider-more-radi cal-more-break.

Cant, C. (2018c) '#Slaveroo: An interview with Belgian riders', *Notes from Below* [Online]. Available at https://notesfrombelow.org/article/slaveroo-belgian-riders.

Cant, C. (2019) *Riding for Deliveroo: Resistance in the New Economy*, Cambridge, Polity.

Cant, C. and Mogno, C. (2020) 'Platform Workers of the World, Unite! The Emergence of the Transnational Federation of Couriers', *The South Atlantic Quarterly*, vol. 119, no. 2, pp. 401–411.

Cederström, C. and Fleming, P. (2012) *Dead Man Working*, Winchester, Zero Books.

Clark, N. and Herman, E. (2017) *Unpaid Britain: wage default in the British Labour Market*, Middlesex University.

Dalla Costa, M. and James, S. (1971) *The Power of Women and the Subversion of the Community*, Brooklyn, NY, Pétroleuse Press.

De Stefano, V. (2019) '"Negotiating the Algorithm": Automation, Artificial Intelligence and Labour Protection', *Comparative Labor Law & Policy Journal*, vol. 41, no. 1.

Deery, S., Iverson, R. and Walsh, J. (2002) 'Work Relationships in Telephone Call Centres: Understanding Emotional Exhaustion and Employee Withdrawal', *Journal of Management Studies*, vol. 39, pp. 471–96.

Doogan, K. (2009) *New Capitalism? The Transformation of Work*, London, Polity.

Doorn, N. and Badger, A. (2020) 'Platform Capitalism's Hidden Abode: Producing Data Assets in the Gig Economy', *Antipode*, vol. 52, no. 5, pp. 1475–1495.

Duggan, J., Sherman, U., Carbery, R. and McDonnell, A. (2020) 'Algorithmic management and app-work in the gig economy: A research agenda for employment relations and HRM', *Human Resource Management Journal*, vol. 30, no. 1, pp. 114–132.

Duménil, G. and Lévy, D. (2005) 'The Neoliberal (Counter-)Revolution', in Saad-Filho, A. and Johnston, D. (eds), *Neoliberalism: A Critical Reader*, London, Pluto Press.

Dunn, S. and Metcalf, D. (1994) 'Trade Union Law since 1978: Ideology, Intent, Impact', Working paper, London, UK: Centre for Economic Performance, London School of Economics.

Englert, S., Woodcock, J. and Cant, C. (2020) 'Digital Workerism: Technology, Platforms, and the Circulation of Workers' Struggles', *tripleC*, vol. 18, no. 1, pp. 132–145.

Fisher, M. (2009) *Capitalist Realism: Is There No Alternative?*, Winchester, Zero Books.

Fredman, S. (2003) 'Women at Work: The Broken Promise of Flexicurity', *Industrial Law Journal*, vol. 33, no. 4, pp. 229–319.

Freeman, R. and Pelletier, J. (1990) 'The Impact of Industrial Relations Legislation on British Union Density', *British Journal of Industrial Relations*, vol. 28, no. 2, pp. 141–164 [Online]. DOI: 10.1111/j.1467-8543.1990.tb00360.x.

Goos, M. and Manning, A. (2007) 'Lousy and Lovely Jobs: The Rising Polarization of Work in Britain', *Review of Economics and Statistics*, vol. 89, no. 1, pp. 118–133.

gov.uk (2022a) *Employing people* [Online]. Available at www.gov.uk/browse/employing-people.

gov.uk (2022b) *Working, jobs and pensions* [Online]. Available at www.gov.uk/browse/working.

Graeber, D. (2016) *The Utopia of Rules: On Technology, Stupidity, and the Secret Joys of Bureaucracy*, London, Melville House Publishing.

Graham, M. and Woodcock, J. (2018) 'Towards a Fairer Platform Economy: Introducing the Fairwork Foundation', *Alternate Routes*, vol. 29, pp. 242–253.

Gray, M.L. and Suri, S. (2019) *Ghost Work: How to Stop Silicon Valley from Building a New Global Underclass*, New York, Houghton Mifflin Harcourt.

Gronroos, C. (1990) *Service Management and Marketing: Managing the Moments of Truth in Service Competition*, Lexington, Lexington Books.

Hardt, M. and Negri, A. (2001) *Empire*, Cambridge, MA, Harvard University Press.

Hardt, M. and Negri, A. (2004) *Multitude: War and Democracy in the Age of Empire*, New York, Penguin.

Harvey, D. (2003) *The New Imperialism*, Oxford, Oxford University Press.

Harvey, D. (2007) *A Brief History of Neoliberalism*, Oxford, Oxford University Press.

Heery, E. (2002) 'Partnership versus Organising: Alternative Futures for British Trade Unionism', *Industrial Relations Journal*, vol. 33, pp. 20–35.

Heery, E.J. (2010) 'Debating employment law: responses to juridification', in Blyton, P.R., Heery, E.J. and Turnbull, P.J. (eds), *Reassessing the Employment Relationship, Management, work and organisations*, London, Palgrave Macmillan, pp. 71–96.

Heskett, J., Sasser Jr., W.E. and Schlesinger, L. (1997) *The Service Profit Chain: How Leading Companies Link Profit and Growth to Loyalty, Satisfaction, and Value*, New York, Free Press.

Hochschild, A.R. (1983) *The Managed Heart: The Commercialisation of Human Feeling*, Berkeley, University of California Press.

Holgate, J. (2021) *Arise: power, strategy and union resurgence*, Wildcat series, London, Pluto Press.

Ibsen, C.L. and Tapia, M. (2017) 'Trade union revitalisation: Where are we now? Where to next?', *Journal of Industrial Relations*, vol. 59, no. 2, pp. 170–191 [Online]. DOI: 10.1177/0022185616677558.

International Labour Organization (2011) *Policies and Regulations to Combat Precarious Employment*, Geneva, International Labour Organization.

Irani, L. and Silberman, M.S. (2013) 'Turkopticon: Interrupting Worker Invisibility in Amazon Mechanical Turk', *Proceedings of CHI 2013*, New York, ACM Press, pp. 611–620.

Joyce, S., Neumann, D., Trappmann, V. and Umney, C. (2020) 'A global struggle: worker protest in the platform economy', *ETUI Policy Brief*, vol. 2 [Online]. Available at www.etui.org/publications/ policy-briefs/european-economic-employment-and-social-policy/a-global-struggle-worker-prot est-in-the-platform-economy.

Kalleberg, A.L. (2009) 'Precarious Work, Insecure Workers: Employment Relations in Transition', *American Sociological Review*, vol. 74, no. 1, pp. 1–22.

Kaplanis, I. (2007) *The Geography of Employment Polarisation in Britain*, London, Institute for Public Policy Research.

Kelly, J. (1998) *Rethinking Industrial Relations: Mobilisation, Collectivism and Long Waves*, London, LSE/ Routledge.

Kessler, S. (2018) *Gigged: The Gig Economy, the End of the Job and the Future of Work*, New York, St. Martin's Press.

Kirk, E. (2020) 'Contesting "bogus self-employment" via legal mobilisation: The case of foster care workers', *Capital & Class*, vol. 44, no. 4, pp. 531–539.

Klein, N. (2008) *The Shock Doctrine: The Rise of Disaster Capitalism*, London, Penguin Books.

Korczynski, M. (2002) *Human Resource Management in Service Work*, Basingstoke, Palgrave.

Lazzarato, M. (1996) 'Immaterial Labour', in Virno, P. and Hardt, M. (eds), *Radical Thought in Italy*, Minneapolis, MN, University of Minnesota Press.

Lee, M.K., Kusbit, D., Metsky, E. and Dabbish, L. (2015) 'Working with machines: The impact of algo-rithmic, data-driven management on human workers', Begole, B., Kim, J., Inkpen, K. and Wood, W. (eds), *Proceedings of the 33rd Annual ACM SIGCHI Conference*, New York, ACM Press.

Lewig, K.A. and Dollard, F. M. (2003) 'Emotional Dissonance, Emotional Exhaustion and Job Satisfaction in Call Centre Workers', *European Journal of Work and Organizational Psychology*, vol. 12, no. 4, pp. 366–92.

Lodge, M. and Hood, C. (2012) 'Into an age of multiple Austerities? Public management and public service bargains across OECD countries', *Governance*, vol. 25, no. 1, pp. 79–101.

London Employment Legal Advice Network (2021) *A Fairer Working London* [Online]. Available at www.trustforlondon.org.uk/publications/fairer-working-london/.

Machin, S. (2000) 'Union Decline in Britain', *British Journal of Industrial Relations*, vol. 38, pp. 631–645.

Machin, S. and Wood, S. (2005) 'Human Resource Management as a Substitute for Trade Unions in British Workplaces', *ILR Review*, vol. 58, no. 2, pp. 201–218 [Online]. DOI: 10.1177/001979390505800202.

Marx, K. (1867) *Capital: A Critique of Political Economy Vol. 1*, 1976, London, Penguin Books.

McAlevey, J. (2016) *No shortcuts: organizing for power in the new gilded age*, New York, Oxford University Press.

McKarthy, K. (2005) 'Is Precarity Enough?', *Mute*, vol. 2, pp. 54–58.

Mirchandani, K. (2012) *Phone Clones: Authenticity Work in the Transnational Service Economy*, London, ILR Press.

Mitropoulos, A. (2005) 'Precari-Us', *Mute: Precarious Reader*, vol. 2, pp. 12–19.

Mogno, C. (2018) 'A new global challenge against platform capitalism', *Notes from Below* [Online]. Available at https://notesfrombelow.org/article/new-global-challenge-against-platform-capitalism.

Munke, R. (2005) 'Neoliberalism and Politics, and the Politics of Neoliberalism', in Saad-Filho, A. and Johnston, D. (eds), *Neoliberalism: A Critical Reader*, London, Pluto.

Murray, G. (2017) 'Union renewal: what can we learn from three decades of research?', *Transfer: European Review of Labour and Research*, vol. 23, no. 1, pp. 9–29 [Online]. DOI: 10.1177/1024258916681723.

Ness, I. (2014) 'Introduction', in Ness, I. (ed), *New Forms of Worker Organization: The Syndicalist and Autonomist Restoration of Class Struggle Unionism*, Oakland, CA, PM Press, pp. 1–17.

OECD (2021) *Government at a Glance 2021*, Government at a Glance, OECD [Online]. DOI: 10.1787/gov_glance-2015-en (Accessed 19 May 2022).

ONS (2022) *Public sector employment, UK: December 2021*, Statistical bulletin, UK, Office for National Statistics [Online]. Available at www.ons.gov.uk/employmentandlabourmarket/peopleinwork/publicsectorpersonnel/bulletins/publicsectoremployment/latest.

Perlin, R. (2012) *Intern nation: earning nothing and learning little in the brave new economy*, Updated paperback ed., London, Verso.

Phelan, C. (ed) (2007) *Trade union revitalisation: trends and prospects in 34 countries*, Oxford, Peter Lang.

Poell, T., Nieborg, D.B. and Duffy, B.E. (2022) *Platforms and cultural production*, Medford, Polity Press.

Pollert, A. and Charlwood, A. (2009) 'The Vulnerable Worker in Britain and Problems at Work', *Work, Employment and Society*, vol. 23, no. 2, pp. 343–362.

Price, R. and Bain, G.S. (1983) 'Union Growth in Britain: Retrospect and Prospect', *British Journal of Industrial Relations*, vol. 21, no. 1, pp. 46–68 [Online]. DOI: 10.1111/j.1467-8543.1983.tb00120.x.

Ritzer, G. (1993) *The McDonaldization of society: an investigation into the changing character of contemporary social life*, Newbury Park, Calif, Pine Forge Press.

Rose, R. (ed) (1985) *Public Employment in Western Nations*, Cambridge, Cambridge University Press.

Rosenblat, A. (2018) *Uberland: How Algorithms are Rewriting the Rules of Work*, Oakland, University of California Press.

Rosenblat, A. and Stark, L. (2016) 'Algorithmic Labor and Information Asymmetries: A Case Study of Uber's Drivers', *International Journal of Communication*, vol. 10, pp. 3758–3784.

Ryan, B. (2005) *Labour Migration and Employment Rights*, Liverpool, Institute of Employment Rights.

Schregle, J. and Jenks, C.W. (2017) 'Labor Law', in *Encyclopaedia Britannica*, Chicago, Encyclopaedia Britannica [Online]. Available at www.britannica.com/topic/labour-law/.

Sherry (2020) 'Living as a Turker: An inquiry at Amazon Mechanical Turk', *Notes from Below* [Online]. Available at https://notesfrombelow.org/article/living-turker (Accessed 24 September 2021).

Silver, B.J. (2003) *Forces of Labor, Workers' Movements and Globalization since 1870*, Cambridge, Cambridge University Press.

Simms, M. and Holgate, J. (2010) 'Organising for what? Where is the debate on the politics of organising?', *Work, Employment and Society*, vol. 24, pp. 157–168.

Srnicek, N. (2017) *Platform Capitalism*, Cambridge, Polity.

Standing, G. (2011) *The Precariat: The New Dangerous Class*, London, Bloomsbury.

Tassinari, A. and Maccarrone, V. (2020) 'Riders on the Storm: Workplace Solidarity among Gig Economy Couriers in Italy and the UK', *Work, Employment and Society*, vol. 34, no. 1, pp. 35–54.

Taylor, P. and Bain, P. (1999) '"An Assembly Line in the Head": Work and Employee Relations in the Call Centre', *Industrial Relations Journal*, vol. 30, no. 2, pp. 101–17.

Vallas, S. and Schor, J.B. (2020) 'What Do Platforms Do? Understanding the Gig Economy', *Annual Review of Sociology*, vol. 46, pp. 273–294.

Waters, F. and Woodcock, J. (2017) 'Far From Seamless: A Workers' Inquiry at Deliveroo', *Viewpoint Magazine* [Online]. Available at www.viewpointmag.com/2017/09/20/far-seamless-workers-inquiry-deliveroo/.

Weber, M. (1930) *The Protestant Ethic and the Spirit of Capitalism*, London, Unwin Hyman.

Woodcock, J. (2017) *Working the Phones: Control and Resistance in Call Centres*, London, Pluto.

Woodcock, J. (2020) 'The Algorithmic Panopticon at Deliveroo: Measurement, Precarity, and the Illusion of Control', *Ephemera*, vol. 20, no. 3, pp. 67–95.

Woodcock, J. (2021) *The Fight Against Platform Capitalism: An Inquiry into the Global Struggles of the Gig Economy*, London, University of Westminster Press.

Woodcock, J. (2022) 'Artificial intelligence at work: The problem of managerial control from call centers to transport platforms', *Frontiers in Artificial Intelligence*, vol. 5 [Online]. DOI: 10.3389/frai.2022.888817 (Accessed 28 October 2022).

Woodcock, J. and Graham, M. (2019) *The Gig Economy: A Critical Introduction*, Cambridge, Polity.

CHAPTER 5

RESEARCHING EMPLOYMENT

So far in this book, the focus has been on different ways to understand and theorise employment. This has covered the histories, geographies, and ways of managing, as well as the contemporary dynamics of work. This chapter will move on to discuss how employment can be researched. It introduces different ways to research employment, including through quantitative data, surveys, interviews, ethnography, digital methods, and more. This is not intended to be a replacement for a method textbook, instead discussing the specifics of these different methods for their application and use in research on employment. There are many excellent methods textbooks, including *Bryman's Social Research Methods* (Clark et al., 2021) and many methodological or methods-focused academic journals.

Methods, as anyone who has been a student in (or indeed been taught) methods classes in universities, is not always considered the most exciting topic. Often it focuses on the intricacies of the process, warning about the risks, and ways of calculating regression analysis and so on. However, this misses why methods can be so important – and even exciting. As I have argued elsewhere:

> Whenever I explain what my own work involves … I shorten it to say: 'my work is researching work.' This is met with a range of responses: sometimes a lack of interest (an important reminder to researchers that while our topic may be the most important thing to us, other people may not care at all), feigning interest ('oh sounds interesting'), a joke about academia (the best involving some kind of comment about how that can be 'real' work), or spark the start of a conversation about how work is changing. However, my work being about researching work is only one part of the story. Social research has the challenge of involving the researcher being a part of what they are trying to understand. There is no chemistry set of workers and capital that can be objectively experimented with. Instead, researchers interested in work have to make sense of their own work in relation to the work they are researching.
>
> (Woodcock, 2021)

Learning how to effectively research employment is a skill that can be very useful for academic pursuits. It may help you get the marks you want for an essay or dissertation. However, it can also be important much more widely.

Before, alongside, and/or after your studies you are likely to have to work. Work, as discussed in other chapters, is an activity that most of us will spend the vast majority of our time doing. The moment we start work, we have to try and figure out what is expected of us, what the norms and rules of the workplace are, or how the organisation works. This can be a simple as working out when and where to take the best breaks, what the options for lunch are, who is influential in the workplace, to much more complicated issues like how to get a promotion or a pay rise. We might do some background research on a company before applying, speak to people who work there, or try to make sense of our first day. Each of these involve informal practices of research methods that will be discussed in this chapter. A more thorough and critical understanding of methods can help make the most of our experiences and equip us to understand employment much more widely.

You may have your own experiences of work that you can bring to thinking about employment. If not, you are likely planning to find some sort of employment after you graduate. If you do not have direct experience yourself, it is worth thinking about the kinds of employment that your family and friends are involved in. The aim of this chapter is to break down methods with practical examples, as well as classic and influential studies, to explore what methods you could

DOI: 10.4324/9781003279907-6

use. This could be inspiration for research to be carried out for a student project, for further studies, or to think critically about the world of work.

The first part of this chapter discusses the history of different ways to research employment. It then starts with the first part of the research process: thinking about what kinds of questions to be asked. It then considers the issue of research ethics, particularly in relation to employment. The rest of the chapter moves through a theoretical and practical discussion of different methods. First, quantitative methods, including surveys and secondary data analysis. Second, qualitative approaches, including interviews and ethnography. The chapter finishes with a reflection on digital methods and why research on employment is important.

A BRIEF HISTORY OF RESEARCHING EMPLOYMENT

There is a very long history of attempting to research work, almost as long as there has been employment. Some of the earliest research into work in the UK was conducted in 1086, almost a millennia ago. The Domesday Book compiled detailed information on the numbers of settlements in counties, the plough teams per settlement, rural population in households – and the percentage of which who were obligated landowners and slaves – the number of churches, and so on. The key reason for conducting this inquiry was to determine the taxes that had been owed during the reign of Edward the Confessor. William the Conqueror wanted to understand power and ownership, as well as reasserting the rights of the Crown.

The survey had an apocalyptic title. As Richard FitzNeal, the treasurer of England under the rule of Henry II, explained:

> The book is metaphorically called by the native English, Domesday, i.e., the Day of Judgement. For as the sentence of that strict and terrible last account cannot be evaded by any skilful subterfuge, so when this book is appealed to on those matters which it contains, its sentence cannot be quashed or set aside with impunity. That is why we have called the book 'the Book of Judgement'''[Domesday], not because it contains decisions on various difficult points, but because its decisions, like those of the Last Judgement, are unalterable.
>
> (Johnson, 1983, 64)

A similar project, the *Catalogus Baronum*, was undertaken by the Normans in Southern Italy. Nothing on this scale was attempted in Britain until the 1873 Return of Owners of Land. This 'Modern Domesday' (Hoskins, 1972, 87), had much less about work, instead focusing on (as the name suggests) land ownership.

Alongside this, national censuses in Britain started in 1801. These had a broader interest that encompassed aspects of employment. Each household was asked for the number of people occupied in agriculture, or in trade, manufacture, or handicraft. We know that it was approximately two million in each. There was no detail about the work involved or the experience of it. The censuses continued almost every ten years after that. John Rickman led the campaign for the first census (and indeed oversaw the first four censuses). He provided 12 reasons for why carrying out a census would benefit a country, which ranged from 'military matters to concerns about food supply, but at the forefront of his philosophy was his statement that "the intimate knowledge of any country must form from the rational basis of legislation and diplomacy"' (Christian and Annal, 2014, 6). He was similarly interest in work, but because 'an industrious population is the basic power and resource of any nation, and therefore its size needs to be known' (Christian and Annal, 2014, 6).

The census is one example of the imperative for governments to investigate populations, including work and employment. A year after the first census, the Health and Morals of Apprentices Act 1802 was introduced. In response to concerns raised in Manchester over the conditions of children employed in the cotton mills, the Act sought to introduce regulations to improve conditions. The enforcement was left up to local magistrates, but it did not require them to intervene. Manchester, as a city at the heart of the industrial revolution, became a focus for understanding changes in employment. The textile industry in Manchester was drawing large numbers of people in from the countryside to new conditions in factories. The draw of the factory also brought others into the city, including Friedrich Engels in 1842. As David McLennan explained in his preface, Engels 'decided to unite his business career and political interest by going to work … in his father's factory' (Engels, 1844, xii).

In Manchester, Engels met Mary Burns, who introduced him to the people who worked and lived in the working-class neighbourhoods. Unlike the surveys that had come before, Engels undertook an ethnographic project that was published as *The Conditions of the Working Class in England*. As he explained:

> I wanted more than a mere abstract knowledge of my subject, I wanted to see you in your own homes, to observe you in your everyday life, to chat with you on your conditions and grievances, to witness your struggles against the social and political power of your oppressors.
>
> (Engels, 1844, xiii)

What Engels found was conditions that were 'the highest and most unconcealed pinnacle of social misery existing in our day' (Engels, 1844, 12).

As a side note, we can also see the changes in Manchester with employment starkly today. At the heart of a district that once housed factory workers, there is now a statue memorialising Engels. The neighbourhood has changed much in the intervening years. Many buildings and forms of work have come and gone, while Engels now stands outside of HOME, a performing arts venue, rather than industrial workplaces and slum housing.

Engels would also invite Karl Marx to visit him in Manchester during this time. A few years later, they wrote *The Communist Manifesto* together (Marx and Engels, 1848). When Marx later wrote *Capital* (Marx, 1867), chapter ten focused on a similar kind of ethnographic detail to Engels, including the 'massive use of empirical evidence' (Kincaid, 2008, 388). However, unlike Engels, Marx would rely on research carried out by others to understand work. In particular, Marx relied on evidence produced by factory inspectors. Indeed, as David Harvey has argued, he 'would not have been able to write this Chapter without the abundant information they supplied' (Harvey, 2010, 141). Marx also writes that 'the "ruthless" factory inspector Leonard Horner was again on the spot' and how 'his services to the English working class will never be forgotten' (Marx, 1867, 397). These factory inspectors were civil servants who acted on the orders of the state – clearly having a different starting point to either Marx or Engels. David Harvey explains that the factory inspectors were introduced because of a combination of 'bourgeois morality and the military concerns of the state' (Harvey, 2010, 142). There are some similarities to the concerns that encouraged the first surveys, as well as the 'strong currents of bourgeois reformism' that were present at the time (Harvey, 2010, 142).

Marx would later try and undertake his own research into the experience of work. In his 'call for a workers' inquiry', he outlined a set of questions to be circulated to workers. In the introduction, he explains:

> We hope to meet in this work with the support of all workers in town and country who understand that they alone can describe with full knowledge the misfortunes from which they suffer, and that only they, and not saviors sent by Providence, can energetically apply the healing remedies for the social ills to which they are a prey.
>
> (Marx, 1880)

This is clearly a different project to undertaking national surveys or inspecting factories. Workers are not considered as passive subjects to be researched or offer up data, instead they are considered as both the only people who can explain their conditions and be able to transform them. As Marx continues, those doing an inquiry 'must wish for an exact and positive knowledge of the conditions in which the working class – the class to whom the future belongs – works and moves' (Marx, 1880). There are some similarities here with other academic approaches, including history from below as a people's history – rather than a study of elites (Thompson, 1991), women's history (Rowbotham, 1977), or subaltern studies (Spivak, 1988).

The reason to draw attention to these different approaches is that even in those kinds of research that are sympathetic to the conditions of factory workers in the 19th century in Britain, there are a range of different kinds of investigations, undertaken for differing reasons. This does not include those studies carried out explicitly to intensify production on behalf of factory owners themselves. While many years have now passed, it is still worth thinking about how the different interests involved with employment have an important bearing on the kinds of research that is, and can be, done. For example, research may start from the interests of workers, employers, or the state. There may be points where the interests of the state side entirely with the employers, or other points in which they are more sympathetic to workers.

RESEARCH QUESTIONS FOR UNDERSTANDING EMPLOYMENT

Before going on to discuss the different methods that can be used to research employment, it is first worth exploring what kinds of questions can be asked. Good research begins with a strong research question. There are three ways in which research questions can be judged. First, a question for which the answer matters. The answer is therefore consequential and can tell us something important. Second, that the question builds upon an existing body of knowledge and extends our understanding. It is therefore novel and involves something new. Third, that the question is feasible to answer – or at least partially answer. This means the answer can be valid, both in terms of being relevant and generating knowledge.

Good research questions therefore need to be researchable. They have to provide a starting point for a project to investigate. Although they may be researchable, it is important that they do not have an easy answer. This opens up a process through which they can be investigated through multiple sources and angles, and may even throw up other questions which can be included along the way. The questions may be motivated by words like 'how', 'why', or 'which' that point the research in a certain direction. On the other hand, bad research questions often have simple and easy answers. If someone can easily answer the research question without undertaking any research (and this may just be responding 'no'), then it may well not be worth pursuing. Similarly, a bad question may have no answer as it is not framed in the way that it can be addressed.

As Gary Marx observes, 'one of the wonders' of doing research 'is the freedom to choose what you will study' (Marx, 1997, 113). He continues to outline a series of 'sources' for research questions, which can also be considered in relation to employment specifically (Marx, 1997, 113–114):

- 'Intellectual puzzles and contradictions'. You may have come across a paradox related to employment that can generate useful research questions. For example, 'Why does this kind of employment exist in the way it does?'
- 'The literature'. There is a very wide range of existing research on employment, both in the fields of management and more widely. Many journal articles will deliberately indicate avenues for future research (and not only so they can lay the groundwork for their next submission).

- 'Replication'. Existing research can be repeated by applying the approach in a different location, context, timeframe, institution, or so on.
- 'Structures and functions'. You can identify a social structure (of which there are many involved with employment), then consider what explanations there are for the different types of those structures and what effects they have.
- 'Opposition'. Questions can be generated through criticism of existing research. Marx notes that 'you may find a ... perspective or work wrong, troubling, and even anger-provoking'. Starting with a critique of the empirical, theoretical, or even moral grounds of existing research can sharpen the focus for a future project.
- 'A social problem or an unrealized value'. An injustice can provide the impetus for research questions that examine a problem, the causes, effects, and solutions. In the context of employment, there is a long history of critical research that investigates exploitation and detrimental working conditions, alongside a wide range of other problems.
- 'Gaps between official version of reality and facts on the ground'. Often these differences between formal and informal can be a starting point for questions. Most employment involves differences between what is outlined in the contract, the expectations, and the reality of the experience of work. Unpacking how and why these differences emerge, as well as how meaning is made and communicated with respect to employment can be generative here.
- 'The counter-intuitive'. Common sense is not always empirically accurate or helpful for developing research. Thought experiments that cut across received wisdom can provide an interesting starting point for a research question.
- 'Empirical examples that trigger amazement'. There is a very wide range of different types and forms of employment, with many atypical examples. Finding a particularly interesting case, anomaly, or surprising example can provide a great starting point.
- 'New methods and theories'. You may find a new approach, either with a method or ideas, that can be applied to an existing research problem. This can generate new insights both for the focus of the research, as well as learning about the practice of the new methods or theories.
- 'New social and technical developments and social trends'. Changes both within and beyond employment provide the opportunity to inquire into the causes, forms, and consequences of change. While often the focus is on technological change, there are many other processes of change that can be examined in relation to employment.
- 'Personal experience'. You can consider how your own experience of employment (or the employment of people you know) can provide a starting point for a research question.
- 'Sponsors and teachers'. Those you work with (or for) can also provide a starting point for research questions, topics, or direction. There are benefits to taking direction this way, however there are also risks. As Marx notes 'what is troubling is the student who loses autonomy through the colonization of his or her personality by a mentor or the hired gun who is indiscriminate, working for whomever pays the most, regardless of interest in the project or value considerations'. The risk is that research, as employed and directed by someone else, becomes 'alienated labor and eventually may affect the quality of your work and your mental health' (Marx, 1997, 114).

Before embarking on a research project on employment, it is therefore worth spending some time thinking and exploring what sorts of questions can and should be asked.

It is also worth remembering that research is always limited by the resources available. This may include the time of people undertaking it, the skills and capabilities, the budget, and so on.

- An undergraduate project. This may have very limited time, maybe only a month or so, as well as no budget to undertake research. It will likely be an individual project and that limits the scope. It is better to do something simpler well, than try to take on something too complex.
- A Masters dissertation. As with an undergraduate project, this is likely to be an individual research project and will be limited by a shorter timeframe. Similarly, there is likely no budget for the research. However, given the increased academic level, it is expected that the project will engage more critically with the existing literature.
- A PhD project. This is a longer student research project that may be three years or longer. This provides more time (although it may not feel like it in practice) to critically explore the literature.
- A small university research project. Academics may undertake a small research project with some funding to carry out the work, and perhaps 'buying out' some of their time to do it, reducing their teaching and/or admin. This may involve other researchers and outputs for the project – usually journal articles.
- A large university research project. Funding councils like the ESRC (Economic and Social Research Council) that are part of UKRI (United Kingdom Research and Innovation) give large research grants on a competitive basis. These can be hundreds of thousands or even millions of pounds and may last multiple years. Often the focus is on 'buying out' time for a team of researchers and providing a budget to undertake a substantial piece of research.
- Something different. Not all research takes place in the context of a university and there may be very different expectations and requirements for the research. For example, this could be research with a government agency, a charitable sector organisation, or a company.

The main thing to remember is that every piece of research has limitations. Take, for example, any journal article that has ever been written. Each has a word limit that places overall limitations on which topics can be covered and how much detail it can go into. Although books are much longer, they still have limitations on how much can be included. Research is therefore always both about what the researcher chooses to do as well as what they have decided not to do. The strongest explanations or justifications of projects are those that take the limitations seriously and then consider what contribution can be made from the project as it exists.

It is possible to get a sense of whether a research question (or indeed a project) will work in practice by trying to summarise it to other people. As Patrick Dunleavy has argued, this can be summarised in the 'dinner party test', that 'If you cannot give a synoptic, ordinary language explanation in two or three minutes of what you are focusing on and what you hope to achieve, the chances are very high that in very fundamental way you do not yet understand your thesis topic' (Dunleavy, 2003, 22). An interesting or striking research question is a great way to introduce a project in a few sentences. However, this test is also useful for thinking about whether a topic can and should be researched. Firstly, whether something 'can' be researched involves whether participants can be found, data can be accessed, and/or if it can be achieved with available time, effort, and budget. Secondly, whether something 'should' be researched. This is a much broader – and often harder – question to answer. 'Should' can involve a value judgement about whether the research adds to our existing knowledge, reaches an audience, or achieves some other goals.

It is also important to think about the wider narrative of the research. Of course, it is necessary to have a clear research question. Explaining why it is important and interesting is key – particularly if trying to convince someone else to fund the research. It should be in conversation with the existing literature, identifying gaps or problems that can be addressed. The research will involve a theoretical framework that will make sense of and attempt to explain the data. There are many different theoretical frameworks available for research – and the same is true for research on employment. This is not often discussed as part of methods per se, but it is methodologically important to think about how both the epistemology (the theory of how knowledge is generated) and ontology (the concepts and categories used to make sense of the world) relate to a research project and the questions being posed.

RESEARCH ETHICS

The ethics of research is an important consideration, but one that is often narrowly conceived in a university context. Often, ethics is boiled down to the requirement to apply to an ethics committee or other institutional body and get 'sign off' for a project. However, it is worth thinking about the wider ethics of doing research, particularly in the context of employment. Most research on employment will involve collecting data from people, about people, or that could impact people. While this is true of social research more widely, for employment this also means people that are engaged in the process and dynamics of work.

There are a range of different guidelines for conducting ethical research. The British Sociological Association provides a series of guidelines in the 'Statement of Ethical Practice' (BSA, 2017, 5). As it explains, researchers have 'a responsibility to ensure that the physical, social and psychological well-being of research participants is not adversely affected by the research'. This means protecting 'the rights of those they study, their interests, sensitivities and privacy, while recognising the difficulty of balancing potentially conflicting interests' (BSA, 2017, 5).

Research should be designed so that it can protect participants, develop trust, and guard against misconduct or harm. An important principle for this is the idea of 'informed consent'. This means that participation in research:

> should be based on the freely given informed consent of those studied. This implies a responsibility … to explain in appropriate detail, and in terms meaningful to participants, what the research is about, who is undertaking and financing it, why it is being undertaken, and how it is to be distributed and used.
>
> (BSA, 2017, 5)

In part, these guidelines emerged because of unethical research carried out in the past. For example, the Tuskegee Syphilis Study, in which almost 400 African American men with syphilis were studied while leaving the disease untreated. The participants were not informed of the aims of the study and more than 100 died by the end of the study, despite the disease being treatable (Reverby, 2009). In another example, the Milgram Shock Experiment, participants were instructed to obey an authority figure to administer electric shocks. They were told they were participating in another study and participants suffered from high levels of stress in the process. Critics noted that alongside the deception the researchers failed to ensure the well-being of participants (Baumrind, 1964). In terms of research in employment, there have been a series of scandals with researchers working with employers. For example, in The Uber Files it was revealed that Uber 'paid prominent academics hundreds of thousands of dollars to produce research that supported the company's claims about the benefits of its economic model' (Davies et al., 2022).

The goal of a University Ethics Committee is therefore to ensure that risks to subjects are minimised, that risks to participants are reasonable in relation to anticipated benefits, selection of participants is fair, informed consent is sought and documented from each participant, privacy and confidentially is protected, that there are safeguards for vulnerable participants, and that the project makes provisions for data collection, processing, and storage. A further concern is often the legal liability of the university itself. In practice, this means ensuring that participants have access to a 'participant information sheet', that explains the project and provides contact details; can read and sign an informed consent sheet that clearly explains how and why data is being collected; ensures the confidentiality of data collected; and provides anonymity for participants and organisations. This may involve the use of pseudonyms and other ways of preventing the identification of participants.

These formal processes are only one part of designing and carrying out ethical research. Gaining effective informed consent is not a single point in the research project. Instead, it needs to be considered as a part of a process that runs throughout the research, both before, during, and after the data collection takes place. Wider questions also need to be asked about the research, for example, why is this research being undertaken? Who benefits from it? What do the funders want to gain from the research? All research aligns with interests of some kind, whether that of the researcher, the funder, the institutions involved, or with the different power relations involved in the research site.

COLLECTING DATA

Before discussing the different ways that data can be collected, it is first worth thinking about how and why data is being collected. There should be a consideration of the credibility of the research design, particularly in how reliable and valid data can be produced. This is the extent to which the data collection technique or techniques will result in consistent findings, similar observations, have transparency in how sense was made from the data, and reach conclusions.

In some contexts, this can involve test and retest reliability. This means assessing reliability by having the test repeated. If the same 'thing' is measured twice and has the same result, then it is likely to be reliable. However, there may be errors or biases from either participant or researcher that could result in different findings. Often in quantitative (or more positivistic) approaches, the aim is to try and reduce these biases as much as feasible and produce reliable results. However, in qualitative approaches, it may be that reflexivity provides a way to use these biases and subjectivity as part of the research process.

Validity concerns whether the data collection method actually measures what it is intending to measure. This can be more complex than reliability, as it may involve epistemological or ontological issues. This is important for research because the findings need to reflect what they are aiming to explore or explain. Broadly speaking, there are two kinds of validity. The first is internal validity, which refers to the whether the design of the methods measures what they intend to. Making sure the design is valid is an important step in choosing and applying methods. External validity refers to whether the results can be generalised beyond the project or study. For data to be valid, it is necessary for it to be reliable. However, reliability on its own is not enough for validity.

Considering these different factors for research design can be an important first step before choosing which methods to use. For example, after designing research questions, considering the ethics, and thinking about what kinds of data will be needed for the study, it then makes sense to choose a method. Starting out from a method – wanting to do an ethnographic study or interview people – means we may miss the opportunity to find reliable and valid by another means.

QUANTITATIVE RESEARCH

Surveys are a widely used way to collect quantitative data (Fowler, 2001). They have been widely used to study employment, as discussed earlier in this chapter. Effective surveys are difficult and costly to undertake as an individual researcher. They require a thoughtful approach to design and the writing of questions. Good surveys require respondents that are willing to answer, will interpret the questions in the same way, and are able to respond accurately. In particular, this means using simple words and phrases, avoiding vague quantifiers (for example, occasionally, which can vary in meaning), and ensure there is a logical flow that runs through the questionnaire.

It is not always necessary to design your own study to collect quantitative data. Secondary data analysis can be a fruitful approach. It allows the use of data 'for a tiny fraction of the resources involved in carrying out a data collection exercise' (Bryman, 2008, 297). Reducing the resource needed at this stage means limited resources can be redeployed in the study. For example, the 'approach to the analysis of data can be more considered than perhaps it might otherwise have been' and can allow for new interpretations, even such that 'may not have been envisaged by the original researchers' (Bryman, 2008, 299).

In terms of quantitative datasets relating to employment, there are a range of resources available to researchers. Of course, there is the census data discussed earlier in the chapter. This often has detailed information about the occupation of people across the country, even down to granular local level. For example, the Office for National Statistics (ONS) is the national statistical institute for the UK. They collect statistics related to the economy, population, and society, many of which are relevant for studying employment. They are also responsible for carrying out the census in England and Wales every ten years. Nomis, a service provided by the Office for National Statistics, provides access to many datasets. It provides a relatively straightforward way to access labour market statistics, local area reports (by postcode or area name), query data, and browse the census statistics. In particular, Nomis provides access to the following datasets outlined in Table 5.1 (Nomis, 2022).

Table 5.1 Nomis Datasets

Data Source	Description
Annual Civil Service Employment Survey	A count of home Civil Service employees. It excludes the Northern Ireland Civil Service, other Crown servants and employees in the wider public sector, for example, employees of Non-Departmental Public Bodies (NDPBs) and the National Health Service (NHS).
Annual Population Survey / Labour Force Survey	A residence-based labour market survey encompassing population, economic activity (employment and unemployment), economic inactivity, and qualifications. These are broken down where possible by gender, age, ethnicity, industry, and occupation. Available at Local Authority level and above. Updated quarterly.
Annual Survey of Hours and Earnings	Conducted in April each year to obtain information about the levels, distribution and make-up of earnings and hours worked for employees. ASHE is based on a sample of employee jobs taken from HM Revenue & Customs PAYE records. Information on earnings and hours is obtained in confidence from employers. ASHE does not cover the self-employed nor does it cover employees not paid during the reference period.
Business Register and Employment Survey / Annual Business Inquiry	An employer survey of the number of jobs held, broken down by industry. BRES publishes employee and employment estimates at detailed geographical and industrial levels and is the official source of employee and employment estimates by detailed geography and industry.
Census of Population	Census data from the 1961, 1981, 1991, 2001, and 2011 Census.

Table 5.1 (Cont.)

Data Source	Description
Claimant Count	This experimental series counts the number of people claiming Jobseeker's Allowance plus those who claim Universal Credit and are required to seek work and be available for work and replaces the number of people claiming Jobseeker's Allowance as the headline indicator of the number of people claiming benefits principally for the reason of being unemployed.
DWP Benefits	Data in this section are supplied by the Department for Work and Pensions and provide a snapshot of benefit claimants at particular points in time.
Jobs density	The numbers of jobs per resident aged 16–64. The total number of jobs is a workplace-based measure and comprises employees, self-employed, government-supported trainees, and HM Forces.
Jobseekers Allowance	Data in this section includes the number of people claiming Jobseeker's Allowance (JSA) and National Insurance credits at Jobcentre Plus local offices. Jobseeker's Allowance datasets only cover a subset of people claiming unemployment related benefits. For data on all people claiming benefits principally for the reason of being unemployed please use the Claimant Count series.
Life events	Data in this section includes marriages, divorces, births, and mortality.
Population Estimates / Projections	The midyear (30 June) estimates of population are based on results from the latest Census of Population with allowance for under-enumeration. Available at Local Authority level and above.
Regional accounts	Includes Regional gross disposable household income (GDHI) and Regional gross value added.
UK Business Counts	Includes UK Business Counts for enterprises and local units.
Workforce Jobs	Workforce Jobs (WFJ) is a quarterly measure of the number of jobs in the UK and is the preferred measure of the change in jobs by industry. Estimates are only available at national and regional level.
Archived	
Jobcentre Plus Vacancies	This series was discontinued in 2012. Data in this section was supplied by the Department for Work and Pensions and provided information about vacancies notified by employers to Jobcentre Plus.
VAT Registrations & Stocks	This series was discontinued in 2007.

Source: Adapted from Nomis, 2022

There is also the UK Data Service that is funded by the UKRI and curates and provides access to research data. It includes 1,728 studies and 28 data series on the topic of 'labour and employment' (UK Data Service, 2022). Table 5.2 provides a selection of data series that may be useful for research into employment.

There are equivalent or similar datasets for other countries, although there may be differences in the scale, granularity, and methodology for collecting data. There are also international datasets and comparisons that can be utilised in some cases too. For example, the OECD Employment and Labour Market statistics (OECD, 2022).

Table 5.2 UK Data Service

Data Source	Description
Understanding Society	The Understanding Society study, or the United Kingdom Household Longitudinal Study (UKHLS), which began in 2009, is conducted by the Institute for Social and Economic Research (ISER), at the University of Essex. As a multi-topic household survey, the purpose of Understanding Society is to understand social and economic change in Britain at the household and individual levels. It is anticipated that over time the study will permit examination of short-term and long-term effects of social and economic change, including policy interventions, on the general well-being of the UK population.
1970 British Cohort Study	The 1970 British Cohort Study (BCS70) follows the lives of more than 17,000 people born in England, Scotland, and Wales in a single week of 1970. Over the course of cohort members' lives, the BCS70 has broadened from a strictly medical focus at birth to collect information on health, physical, educational and social development, and economic circumstances among other factors. The BCS70 is conducted by the Centre for Longitudinal Studies (CLS).
Next Steps (previously the Longitudinal Study of Young People in England)	Next Steps (also known as the Longitudinal Study of Young People in England (LSYPE1)) is a major longitudinal study that follows the lives of around 16,000 people born in 1989–1990 in England. The first seven sweeps of the study (2004–2010) were funded and managed by the Department for Education (DfE) and mainly focused on the educational and early labour market experiences of young people. The study began in 2004 and included young people in Year 9 who attended state and independent schools in England. Following the initial survey at age 13–14, the cohort members were interviewed every year until 2010.
United Kingdom Time Use Survey	The United Kingdom Time Use Surveys were conducted in 2000–2001 and 2014–2015. The 2014–2015 survey was conducted by NatCen and designed to be, as far as possible, compatible both with the 2000–2001 survey (conducted by the Office for National Statistics) and with other European time use studies carried out since 2008 (not currently held at the UK Data Service). The 2014–2015 study was deposited by the Centre for Time Use Research at the University of Oxford. The main aim of the surveys was to measure the amount of time spent by the population on various activities.
British Social Attitudes Survey	The British Social Attitudes (BSA) survey series, which began in 1983, is designed to produce annual measures of attitudinal movements to complement information gathered from a) large-scale government surveys that deal largely with facts and behaviour patterns, and b) party political attitudes data produced by the polls. One of the main purposes of the BSA is to monitor patterns of continuity and change, and examine the relative rates at which social attitudes change over time.

Table 5.2 (Cont.)

Data Source	Description
Workplace Employment Relations Survey	The Workplace Employment Relations Survey (WERS), (formerly the Workplace Industrial Relations Survey, or WIRS), began in 1980. The series is sponsored by the Economic and Social Research Council (ESRC), government departments, and other organisations and the purpose of each survey has been to provide large-scale, statistically reliable evidence about a broad range of employment practices across almost every sector of the economy. To that end WERS collects information from managers with responsibility for employment relations or personnel matters, employee representatives, and employees themselves.
European Company Survey	The European Company Survey (ECS), (formerly the Establishment Survey on Working Time and Work-Life Balance (ESWT)), aims to map working time policies and practices at the level of the establishment in the European Union and to survey the views of the different actors at establishment level on these policies and practices. It is conducted by a European Union body, the European Foundation for the Improvement of Living and Working Conditions (Eurofound).
European Working Conditions Survey	The European Working Conditions Survey (EWCS) provides an overview on the state of working conditions throughout Europe, as well as indicating the nature and content of changes affecting the workforce and the quality of work.

Source: Adapted from UK Data Service, 2022

INTERVIEWS

A common method for collecting qualitative data on employment is interviewing. Arguably, interviews may be the most common primary research method in management research. Interviews, like other methods, can be used on their own or as part of a broader research project. Indeed, ethnography usually involves interviewing of some kind, whether formal or informal. The same is usually true with case studies or other forms of action research. Almost all managers use a version of the method in their own practice – whether in recruitment interviews, management meetings, or disciplinary investigations. Interviewing already plays an important role in employment.

Interviews can be thought of as a guided conversation. They are a development of the kinds of conversations we have throughout our lives in which we try to make sense of the world. Think about the first encounter you had at a workplace, university, or other organisation you have been involved in. Often, this starts with information sent remotely, but at some stage there will have been conversations in which questions were asked or answers provided. These conversations help us to make sense of the social world, including what we need to do, gauging social norms, or even just figuring out where people go for lunch and what time they leave.

A research interview develops a conversation into a dialogue with an objective: to elicit information from an interviewee (Rowley, 2010). It provides a way to access information that might not be easily accessible to a researcher from the outside. The interview also provides the opportunity to access different interpretations and views of interviewees on a topic or issue. This can investigate how people make sense of their employment, narratives they make about it, or their beliefs and values. Interviews can be a moment of co-construction that the researcher actively participates in (Holstein and Gubrium, 1995).

In the context of employment, interviews are likely to be used to try and understand an aspect of work. Given the ways in which work becomes enmeshed with workers' lives, there is ample opportunity to engage with how sense is made of work, or the meanings attached to it. Work is a social relationship. Therefore, an interview 'aims to map and understand the respondents' life world ... the objective is a fine-textured understanding of beliefs, attitudes, values and motivations in relation to the behaviours of people in particular social contexts' (Bauer and Gaskell, 2000, 39).

Broadly speaking, there are three kinds of interviews. The first are structured interviews. These involves a clear list of questions – hence they are 'structured' – in which the aim is to collect a standardised set of responses for interviewees. The interview is standardised to attempt to avoid differences in the interview due to the researcher. Often this means specific questions that are read out exactly, likely asking closed questions for interviewees. In this way, it is closer to a survey, carried out live by an interviewer.

There are two kinds of less structured interviews. The first are unstructured, which involves no pre-formulated questions. There may be prompts or topics to follow, but this form of interview is much closer to a conversation. There is no attempt to maintain consistency, like with structured interviews. The conversation is also driven more by the interviewee, who can choose to take it in different directions. These kinds of interviews can produce rich accounts and allow for very detailed understandings to be developed. However, they are also very challenging to conduct and require experienced interviewers to ensure that they can produce data that is useful for the research.

A much more common form of interviews are semi-structured interviews. These are the closest to the guided conversations in which the interview prepares an interview guide with pre-formulated questions beforehand. During the interview, these act more like a guide, rather than a strict instruction. The interviewer does not have to follow these and can improvise during the interview. There is more consistency than with unstructured interviews, but they have the benefit of being able to follow up on topics or issues that come up during the interview.

Interviews, regardless of the types discussed before, are conducted in either a formal or informal manner. Formal interviews often involve setting a time and place for the interview, going through informed consent documents, signing forms, recording the interview. These provide an important opportunity to collect data, however it is not always possible to organise interviews in this way during research projects. While being mindful of the need for informed consent, there are also more informal forms of interviews that can be used during research. These may be unstructured but take advantage of the opportunity to have a conversation with an interviewee that might otherwise be missed. They may not be recorded – instead field notes could be taken afterwards.

Regardless of the format, interviews of all these types can be used to great effect in research on employment. Interviews provide a valuable opportunity to see employment through other people's eyes. Given how much of work is about the experiences that are had every day by workers across a range of very different contexts, locations, and forms of organisations, this is particularly important. Interviews have a sensitivity to context and provide a way to understand the narratives that people create about their own work. A deeper understanding of how social processes, both directly connecting to work and more widely around it, can be developed through interviewing participants. This can mean interrogating the taken-for-granted – that for one person are just the mundane aspects of their work – and explore them from another perspective. Moreover, they also provide the interviewer with the chance to encounter unexpected parts of employment, particularly those that might not be visible or noticeable from outside of work.

There are some specific considerations to keep in mind when using interviews for research on employment. In particular, as employment is a relationship that involves dimensions of power, researchers should think carefully about the risks for participants. There may be clauses in the employment contract that try to control what potential participants can say, as well as preventing them from disclosing details beyond the organisation.

There are specific ethical issues that can arise while doing interviews. Many of these are shared with the general ethical concerns discussed earlier, as well as those related to ethnography in the next section. Formal parts of the ethical review process need to be followed and this is often tied into the production of information sheets and informed consent forms for participants. Beyond this, it is important to make sure that an ethical approach is taken with participants. This has specificities with respect to employment. Consider the ethical expectations that participants may have, as well as any risks they may have in participating, particularly in relation to their employment.

In addition to interviews, focus groups can also be used for similar aims. Instead of one interviewee and interviewer, focus groups bring together a group of respondents to participate in the research together (Kandola, 2012). Focus groups are less common in academic research, but they are widely used in marketing research (Stokes and Bergin, 2006). The researcher acts more like a moderator than an interviewer, directing the discussion. The purpose is to collect views on a topic, but it also provides the opportunity to engage with how individuals discuss issues as members of a group. This group discussion format can elicit a variety of views, but it can also generate further opinions and insights as respondents also respond to each other as well as the researcher. Given the large size of the group involved in a focus group, it can present more logistical challenges for arranging the research, as well as capturing and analysing the data. The researcher has less control than during an interview, but there is more control than participant observation or ethnography (discussed in the next section). Given the group dynamics, there are both important opportunities and challenges for using focus groups during research on employment. First, as employment often involves groups and teams, it provides a way to explore those dynamics. Second, because of power relationships involved in employment, these need to be carefully considered for the effect they can have on soliciting opinions, attitudes, or beliefs about work.

ETHNOGRAPHY

There is a long history of using ethnography to research employment. Ethnography can broadly mean two things. First, a research method that entails the extended involvement of the researcher in the social life of those they study. Ethnography is a qualitative method in which the researcher 'immerses him- or herself in a group for an extended period of time, observing behaviour, listening to what is said in conversations both between others and the fieldworker, and asking questions' (Bryman, 2008, 402). Second, it can also mean the written output of the method: an 'ethnography'. The historical roots of the method are found with anthropology, which often meant a researcher travelling to another country and trying to gain access to a group, spending a considerable amount of time (often years) trying to understand their culture. In the context of employment, this involves trying to understand the details and experience of work.

Ethnography is particularly suitable for studying employment because this kind of method is attentive to the experiences, dynamics, identities, and meanings that participants give to their behaviours and activities. Ethnography is:

> continuous with ordinary life. Much of what we seek to find out in ethnography is knowledge that others already have. Our ability to learn ethnographically is an extension of what every human being must do, that is, learn the meanings, norms, patterns of a way of life.
>
> (Hymes, 1996, 16)

This is particularly important to remember with understanding employment. There are already people who spend much of their time doing forms of work, as well as people who have spent their lives developing expertise in process. Employment is a complex phenomenon that often comprises a significant part of individuals' social lives, while also offering a range of opportunities for collecting data. Effective use of the method requires thinking reflexively about the position of the ethnographer in relation to those they are trying to study (Bourdieu and Wacquant, 1992), as well as considering the dialogues between research and subject, process in the local context and beyond it, as well as with theory (Burawoy, 1998).

There are many famous examples of ethnographies of work. There was a vibrant tradition of workplace ethnographies, including *Working for Ford* (Beynon, 1973), *Girls, Wives, Factory Lives* (Pollert, 1981), and *Women on the Line* (Cavendish, 1982). Michael Burawoy published a series of influential ethnographies, including a study in a copper mine (Burawoy, 1972), manufacturing (Burawoy, 1979), factory regimes in different contexts (Burawoy, 1985), and factories in Hungary (Burawoy and Lukás, 1994). There was then a period in which ethnographies of employment became much less common. For example, while research involving 'primary material of academic researchers, firsthand accounts marshalled by journalists and autobiographical testimonies of workers themselves' continued, there were 'multiple factors combined to arrest the proliferation of these ethnographic accounts' from the 1980s (Taylor et al., 2009, 7–8). The larger economic shifts that have been discussed throughout this book so far, including the relative decline of manufacturing, weakening of trade unions, and lower levels of open struggle, all combined to limit workplace (and specifically factory) ethnographies. However, there has been a return to ethnographies of work in recent years. For example, on low wage work in the USA (Ehrenreich, 2010) and Britain (Bloodworth, 2018), in call centres (Woodcock, 2017), at Deliveroo (Cant, 2019), and many others. As a method it can provide important insights into employment, particularly those that are attentive to the experience of workers and the contradictions in practice.

Ethnography today is not a straightforward approach. There is not one way to 'do' an ethnography. The diversity of experiences of ethnographies leads to many different methodological responses. All ethnographies involve the research being immersed in a social setting for an extended period of time. This means that observations are a key part of ethnography. Indeed, 'participant observation' is another way that this method can be described. However, it may also involve other methods. For example, listening to and engaging in conversations, interviewing, collecting documents, and so on. What is important is that the methods allow the research to develop an understanding of the culture of the group and people's behaviour within the context of that culture. Given the complexity of this, it often involves the writing up of a detailed account of the research.

There are some challenges that need to be considered when undertaking ethnography. These challenges are not always clear from the explanation that academics provide when describing their methods. For example, often 'research accounts in academic journals depart considerably from the research practices of their authors. They offer instead a "reconstructed logic" ... which brings the illusion of order to what is usually a messy and untidy process' (Buchanan et al., 1988, 54). Ethnography is necessarily messy as it involves engaging with the contradictions of the world and people within it.

There are some particular challenges that are worth outlining here. The first is access. This needs to be considered in two ways, both with the research site and the role of the researcher. Research sites can either be 'open' or 'closed' settings. This refers to how they can be accessed. Public spaces are (mostly) open settings, whereas an office or factory is likely to be a closed setting. In general, this can be thought of as closed settings in which you need permission, as opposed to open settings. In reality, of course, there is more of a spectrum, but many sites do fall broadly into one or the other. At the same time, the researchers can be overt about their role,

Table 5.3 Access in Ethnography

	Open setting	Closed setting
Overt researcher	1	4
Covert researcher	2	3

explaining to participants that they are doing research, or they can be covert and not disclose their role (Lugosi, 2006).

There are four broad approaches to gaining access for an ethnography, as illustrated in Table 5.3. An overt researcher in an open setting (1). This involves a researcher that identifies they are doing research in an open setting that does not require permission to access. On the other hand (2) involves not disclosing the role of the researcher. However, open settings are not always as straightforward as they seem. A 'public' setting may allow anyone to formally access them, but there may still be gatekeepers for social groups that may mediate or even prevent access (Monohan and Fisher, 2015; Reeves, 2010). In public settings, 'hanging around' can be an important strategy for gaining access.

On the other hand, closed settings can often require more effort in order to gain access. In the context of employment, this may require negotiation with employers or owners. The process of 'gaining access to most organizational settings is not a matter to be taken lightly but one that involves some combination of, strategic planning, hard work, and dumb luck' (Van Maanen and Kolb, 1985, 11). Access to closed settings can either be achieved through an overt position of the researcher (3), in which negotiation must include disclosure of the research project, or through covert research (4). Workplaces can raise specific challenges for access. This may involve trying to access 'hard to reach jobs', which may be hard to reach 'because management prevent access by researchers, either actively or passively' (Badger and Woodcock, 2019).

Both overt and covert research have ethical concerns (Spicker, 2011). Covert research can reduce the problem of access and participants are less likely to react to the research project. However, it can be harder to take field notes, other methods may not be available, as well involving more complex ethical concerns, and anxiety on the part of the covert researcher. However, it is worth remembering that ethical concerns are not only limited to covert research. If access is negotiated and granted to a closed site, for example, not every person the researcher comes into contact may know that they are an overt researcher. It can be difficult to justify doing covert research and is usually considered as a method of last resort. It is also worth remembering, as Sarsby points out, that:

> every field situation *is* different and initial luck in meeting good informants, being in the right place at the right time and striking the right notes in relationships may be just as important as skill in technique. Indeed, many successful episodes in the field do come about through good luck as much as through sophisticated planning, and many unsuccessful episodes are due as much to bad luck as to bad judgement.
>
> (Sarsby, 1984, 96)

The role of the ethnographer is also an important consideration. There is a sliding scale between involvement and detachment with the role of an ethnographer. At one extreme of involvement is the 'complete participant'. There is then the 'participant-as-observer' and the 'observer-as-participant'. At the other extreme is detachment with the 'complete observer'. Although there is a scale, most researchers would argue that because of the immersive aspect of ethnography and its approach of participant observation, the complete observer role is not appropriate. Any form of social research like this entails some involvement. A passive researcher still participates in the research site by not choosing to engage, which is in itself a form of engagement. Consider how many social settings can be changed by the inclusion of an observer.

The different roles of ethnographers draw attention to an important point of participatory research: the issue of intervention. As Michael Burawoy argues:

> In the positive view participant observation brings insight through proximity but at the cost of distortion. The reflexive perspective embraces participation as intervention precisely because it distorts and disturbs. A social order reveals itself in the way it responds to pressure. Even the most passive observer produces ripples worthy of examination.
>
> (Burawoy, 1998, 16–17)

By entering into a workplace or other setting of employment, the researcher has already made an intervention. Rather than trying to limit the intervention or effect of the researcher/observer, as one might try to do in research from a positive perspective, the intervention can become part of the research process. There are instances where the researcher may have no choice but to get involved, or it may even be part of negotiating access and increasing trust with participants. This can range from taking part in conversations to becoming much more embedded and part of the processes in the research site.

There are further aspects to consider when undertaking an ethnography specifically into employment. Like other forms of ethnography, it will involve the researcher spending an extended period of time immersed in a field site (likely a workplace of some kind), will be led by research questions, and involve the generation of data.

1. Ethnographies of employment are, by definition, focused on the issue of work. The ethnography may be in-person at a workplace, in another site where the work takes place, or it could even be online. The setting will depend on the kind of work being studied.

2. The choice of setting requires a critical engagement with the dynamics of employment. Given the very wide range of different types and forms of employment, this could vary significantly. It may involve learning particularly skills, terminology, or so on. This also requires an awareness of the power dynamics that are present in the workplace, particularly those between employer and employed.

3. Different kinds of employment provide different ways to undertake an ethnography. This includes the kind of work that is involved, but also the range of different activities and behaviours that surround work. Research could focus on an in-depth study of the labour process, the culture of the workplace, dynamics outside of work, and so on. It is important to consider the cultural context in which the employment takes place, with sensitivities towards the different participants.

4. There may be more complex requirements for the participation in some employment contexts than others. While some work takes place in an 'open' setting, much of work happens in 'closed' settings, some of which can be very difficult to effectively access. This may require more resource and costs for some projects in gaining and/or maintaining access.

5. There are always risks that can limit an ethnography in practice. Factors outside of the researcher's control can prevent, limit, or prematurely end access to a research site. There may be constraints on the kinds of data that can be generated or captured, as well as challenges with confidentiality or anonymity. Researchers need to consider any potential problems while planning the project, including backup options should they arise during the research.

6. Particular kinds of data may be difficult to collect during research on employment. Some contexts may be covered by confidentiality or non-disclosure agreements (NDAs), with commercial concerns preventing data from being used. However, there may also be further data collection

methods available to the researcher, including document research (through company records and so on) as well as formal or informal interviews that can supplement the data collection.

7.   There are specific ethical concerns that will be discussed in detail below.

Every form of research involves ethical concerns. With ethnography, there are specific challenges related to the engagement of the research as a participant observer. If the research is conducted from a university, the research project will require ethical approval from an ethics board or some other kind of institutional process. However, it is important to note that ethics is about much more than applications or filling out forms. It is vital that ethnographic researchers consider their role as a researcher and their relationship to the community they are trying to engage with. This is particularly important in the context of employment as many people encountered in this kind of work are involved in the power relationships of work. People may be relying on the work being studied for their livelihood and it may be closely bound up with issues of identity.

Regardless of whether the research is overt or covert, ethnographies often involve encounter other people who may be unable to provide informed consent. These could be people passing through or visiting a research site or involved in some other way that makes it difficult to gain consent. Of course, research should follow ethical guidelines, like those provided by the British Sociological Association discussed earlier (BSA, 2017). Where overt research is carried out, it should be based on the principle of informed consent. In this case, researchers will need to seek formal informed consent, providing information about the research project in an accessible format. Often this means preparing participation sheets and informed consent forms that can be completed by participants.

As noted before, it may not be possible to conduct overt research and the researcher may have to carry out the research covertly. This is not a choice to be taken lightly as:

> There are serious ethical and legal issues in the use of covert research but the use of covert methods may be justified in certain circumstances. For example, difficulties arise when research participants change their behaviour because they know they are being studied. Researchers may also face problems when access to spheres of social life is closed to social scientists by powerful or secretive interests.
>
> (BSA, 2017, 5)

A detailed consideration of the implications and risk of doing covert research is needed. This is not to dissuade researchers from using this method, which has proven an important part of the methodological toolbox, but to ensure that any risks are minimised. It should be considered as a method of last resort and 'should be resorted to only where it is impossible to use other methods to obtain essential data' (BSA, 2017, 5).

In addition to the ethical considerations discussed here, researchers may need to ensure that other disciplinary or institutional guidelines are followed. This may include agreements with research partners or fieldwork sites. It is also worth undertaking a risk assessment that considers the anonymity, privacy, and other work-related issues. Ethics can also cover the research afterwards. The researcher may want to consider what happens with the outputs and whether these can be shared with communities and participants, particularly if there are any benefits from the research.

The process of conducting an ethnography will vary depending on the context and the questions being explored. Unlike other forms of research, sampling can take a very different approach. The research site may be selected for particular reasons, including the possibility of access and the relationship of the site to wider social processes. It is not feasible in ethnography to carry out probability sampling. Often, the sampling of informants is a combination of convenience and snowball sampling. It can take the form of purposive sampling that is non-probability based, instead focusing on a strategic approach to sample those that are relevant to the research questions. This may involve seeking out differences in characteristics, or other factors that help the researcher to answer their questions. Snowball sampling is an approach that involves asking participants to suggest other people to speak to, providing a way to move through contacts based on existing relationships. There can also be a form of theoretical sampling, which is involves a:

> process of data collection for generating theory whereby the analyst jointly collects, codes, and analyses [their] data and decides what data to collect next and where to find them, in order to develop [their] theory as it emerges. The process of data collection is *controlled* by the emerging theory, whether substantive of formal.
>
> (Glaser and Strauss, 1967, 45)

Despite the challenges and complexities discussed so far, it is still necessary to develop a robust approach to the process of data collection in an ethnography. One of the challenges for this is finding a suitable end point to an ethnography. It may be that a project has an obvious end point. For example, the deadline to submit a dissertation or a grant running out. However, it is also worth thinking about when enough data has been generated. This means continuing to collect data, whether through observations, interviews, collecting documents, or so on, until theoretical saturation has been achieved. This is not the final point of understanding everything in minute detail (this is never possible in practice as social settings are subject to constant change). Instead, it means carrying out data collection until the basis of a theory has been formed and confirmed. This means the questions can be addressed and the project can move on to new questions or draw to a close.

A serious methodological concern with ethnography is the validity and the generalisability of the research. As noted earlier with the discussion of the researcher role, the approach for generating knowledge can be quite different with ethnography. Burawoy discusses this in terms of 'engagement', rather than detachment, not seeking an objective form of research (Burawoy, 1998, 5). There are important differences here with a positivistic approach to research that might follow the '4 Rs', that attempt to reduce or eliminate 'reactivity' (that intervention would go against), ensure 'reliability' with case selection, 'replicability' with the potential for subsequent studies to find the same thing, and 'representativeness' in terms of moving from the sample to the whole (Katz, 1983). Instead of following these 'Rs', Burawoy suggests that a reflexive approach can generate a different form of generalisation from an individual ethnographic case. Rather than 'representativeness', we can aim for 'reconstruction'. Instead of trying to move simply between the specific and the general, it involves iterating upon theory, looking not for 'confirmations but refutations that inspire us to deepen that theory' (Burawoy, 1998, 16). This means attempting to reconstruct theory, starting from the idea that in research 'each part contains within it the essential principles of the whole' (Burawoy, 1979, xv). Within the context of employment, it is possible to see these connections from one kind of work to another, whether directly through supply chains or more widely with employment relations.

In practice, much of the research process will involve taking field notes. These may be written in a physical notebook at the time, when there is a moment to take a pause, or at the end of the day. Taking down as much detail as possible provides rich data that can be used in the writing up of the ethnography. These can come in various forms, from mental notes, jotted notes, to full, thick descriptions in field notes. The most effective notes are those that are vivid and clear, bringing to life the research site, not only in what has been observed, but including multisensory accounts of the participation in the research site. After all, the writing up of an ethnography is an attempt to bring to life that research site for readers who have not been able to do the participant observation themselves. As a rule of thumb, if in doubt about whether a note could be useful, write it down.

All research must come to an end. Research questions are posed and then attempts are made to answer them – or the researcher restarts with better questions. The issue of when to stop an ethnography can be a very difficult question. The unstructured nature of this form of research can mean there is no clear end point. However, it does have to come to an end and the research must find a way to exit the research site. This does not have to mean severing all connections and relationships with participants, but there also needs to be a process of writing up, converting notes into the final product. The process of writing up and drafting also provides opportunities (depending on the setting and other constraints) for sharing the ethnography with participants and gathering feedback.

WHY RESEARCH ON EMPLOYMENT MATTERS

This chapter has so far provided an overview of different ways to research employment. As employment is constantly changing, so too are the methods through which we can try to understand it. Each of these methods can be used as part of research projects that you might be considering doing while you are a student. However, many of them can also be useful tools for when you are working. For example, think about the first day at a new job. An understanding of ethnography can help you to make sense of your experiences and how to develop an awareness of how an organisation works. You might also speak to people to try and find things out – interview techniques can help to elicit the information as part of a guided conversation. Much of contemporary work involves research in some way, whether or not it is explicitly discussed as 'research'.

It is also worth noting that there are new ways to carry out research too. For example, during the pandemic, the use of digital communication tools like Zoom became much more widespread. There are now many more online interviews happening than ever before. Digital tools and technologies run across all the methods discussed so far, whether that be in how data is collected, processed, or analysed. Many surveys are now conducted online and after the pandemic, many more interviews are carried out on Zoom, as well as new 'micro-ethnographic moments' (Lyon and Tunåker, 2021). As such:

> Online ethnography is surely a researchers dream. It does not involve leaving the comforts of your office desk; there are no complex access privileges to negotiate; field data can be easily recorded and saved for later analysis; large amounts of information can be collected quickly and inexpensively. A techno-savvy researcher can even automate most of the process of data collection with the right software and artificially semi-intelligence 'bots'. Doubtless Malinowski or Whyte would have been appalled by the ease with which the online version of their craft can be done.
> (Rutter and Smith, 2005, 84)

There are also innovative ways of conducting research beyond digital methods. For example, *The Sociological Review Magazine* hosted an issue on 'Methods and Methodology', including using science fiction writing with Amazon workers (Webb et al., 2021) and more.

Research methods can be adapted and used in new ways to make sense of employment today. This means going out into the world and testing them, whether that is part of a research project, finding out about your own work (or work you might want to do), or for some other curiosity. As a starting point, there are some academic exercises provided at the end of the book.

REFERENCES

Badger, A. and Woodcock, J. (2019) 'Ethnographic Methods with Limited Access: Assessing Quality of Work in Hard to Reach Jobs', in Wheatley, D. (ed), *Handbook of Research Methods on the Quality of Working Lives*, Cheltenham, Edward Elgar, pp. 135–146.

Bauer, M.W. and Gaskell, G. (2000) *Qualitative researching with text, image and sound: a practical handbook*, Los Angeles, SAGE.

Baumrind, D. (1964) 'Some thoughts on ethics of research: After reading Milgram's "Behavioral Study of Obedience."', *American Psychologist*, vol. 19, no. 6, pp. 421–423 [Online]. DOI: 10.1037/h0040128.

Beynon, H. (1973) *Working for Ford*, Harmondsworth, Penguin.

Bloodworth, J. (2018) *Hired: Six Months Undercover in Low-Wage Britain.*, London, Atlantic Books.

Bourdieu, P. and Wacquant, L. (1992) *An Invitation to Reflexive Sociology*, Chicago, University of Chicago Press.

Bryman, A. (2008) *Social Research Methods*, Oxford, Oxford University Press.

BSA (2017) *BSA Statement of Ethical Practice*, The British Sociological Association [Online]. Available at www.britsoc.co.uk/ethics

Buchanan, D., Boddy, D. and McCalman, J. (1988) 'Getting in, getting on, getting out and getting back', in Bryman, A. (ed), *Doing research in organizations*, London, Routledge, pp. 53–67.

Burawoy, M. (1972) *The Colour of Class: From African Advancement to Zambianization*, Manchester, Manchester University Press for the Rhodes-Livingston Institute.

Burawoy, M. (1979) *Manufacturing Consent*, Chicago, IL, University of Chicago Press.

Burawoy, M. (1985) *The Politics of Production*, London, Verso.

Burawoy, M. (1998) 'The Extended Case Method', *Sociological Theory*, vol. 16, no. 1, pp. 4–33.

Burawoy, M. and Lukás, J. (1994) *The Radiant Past: Ideology and Reality in Hungary's Road to Capitalism*, Chicago, University of Chicago Press.

Cant, C. (2019) *Riding for Deliveroo: Resistance in the New Economy*, Cambridge, Polity.

Cavendish, R. (1982) *Women on the Line*, London, Routledge & Paul.

Christian, P. and Annal, D. (2014) *Census: the family historian's guide*, London, Bloomsbury Publishing.

Clark, T., Foster, L., Sloan, L. and Bryman, A. (2021) *Bryman's social research methods*, Sixth edn, Oxford, Oxford University Press.

Davies, H., Goodley, S., Lawrence, F., Lewis, P. and O'Carroll, L. (2022) 'The Uber FIles', *The Guardian*, 11th July [Online]. Available at www.theguardian.com/news/2022/jul/10/uber-files-leak-reveals-global-lobbying-campaign.

Dunleavy, P. (2003) *Authoring a PhD: How to Plan, Draft, Write, and Finish a Doctoral Thesis or Dissertation.*, Basingstoke, Palgrave MacMillan [Online]. Available at https://link.springer.com/book/10.1007/978-0-230-80208-7 (Accessed 16 August 2022).

Ehrenreich, B. (2010) *Nickel and dimed*, London, Granta.

Engels, F. (1844) *The Condition of the Working Class in England*, 2009, Oxford, Oxford University Press.

Fowler, F.J. (2001) *Survey Research Methods*, London, SAGE.

Glaser, B.G. and Strauss, A.L. (1967) *The Discovery of Grounded Theory: Strategies for Qualitative Research*, New York, Aldine Publishing.

Harvey, D. (2010) *A Companion to Marx's Capital*, London, Verso.

Holstein, J. and Gubrium, J. (1995) *The Active Interview*, London, SAGE.

Hoskins, W.G. (1972) *Devon*, Newton Abbot, David and Charles.

Hymes, D. (1996) *Ethnography, Linguistics, Narrative Inequality: Toward An Understanding Of Voice*, London, Taylor and Francis.

Johnson, C. (1983) *Dialogus de Scaccario, the Course of the Exchequer, and Constitutio Domus Regis, The Establishment of the Royal Houshold*, Oxford, Clarendon Press.

Kandola, B. (2012) 'Focus groups', in Symon, G. and Cassell, C.M. (eds), *Qualitative organizational research: core methods and current challenges*, London, Sage, pp. 258–274.

Katz, J. (1983) 'A Theory of Qualitative Methodology: The Social System of Analytical Fieldwork', in Emerson, R. (ed), *Contemporary Field Research*, Illinois, Waveland Press, pp. 127–148.

Kincaid, J. (2008) 'The New Dialectic', in Bidet, J. and Kouvelakis, S. (eds), *Critical Companion to Contemporary Marxism*, Boston, Brill.

Lugosi, P. (2006) 'Between Overt and Covert Research: Concealment and Disclosure in an Ethnographic Study of Commercial Hospitality', *Qualitative Inquiry*, vol. 12, no. 3, pp. 541–561.

Lyon, D. and Tunåker, C. (2021) 'Zoom, Boom! And the Micro-ethnographic Moment', *The Sociological Review Magazine* [Online]. Available at https://thesociologicalreview.org/magazine/november-2021/methods-and-methodology/zoom-boom-and-the-micro-ethnographic-moment/.

Marx, G.T. (1997) 'Of methods and manners for aspiring sociologists: 37 moral imperatives', *The American Sociologist*, vol. 28, no. 1, pp. 102–125 [Online]. DOI: 10.1007/s12108-997-1029-9.

Marx, K. (1867) *Capital: A Critique of Political Economy Vol. 1*, 1976, London, Penguin Books.

Marx, K. (1880) 'A Workers' Inquiry', *New International*, 1938, vol. 4, no. 12, pp. 379–381.

Marx, K. and Engels, F. (1848) *The Communist Manifesto*, [Online]. Available at www.marxists.org/archive/marx/works/1848/communist-manifesto/ch01.htm#007.

Monohan, T. and Fisher, J. (2015) 'Strategies for Obtaining Access to Secretive or Guarded Organizations', *Journal of Contemporary Ethnography*, vol. 44, no. 6, pp. 709–736.

Nomis (2022) *Data Sources* [Online]. Available at www.nomisweb.co.uk/sources (Accessed 18 August 2022).

OECD (2022) *OECD Employment and Labour Market Statistics* [Online]. Available at www.oecd-ilibrary.org/employment/data/oecd-employment-and-labour-market-statistics_lfs-data-en.

Pollert, A. (1981) *Girls, Wives, Factory Lives*, London, Macmillan.

Reeves, C.L. (2010) 'A Difficult Negotiation: Fieldwork Relations with Gatekeepers', *Qualitative Research*, vol. 10, no. 3, pp. 315–331.

Reverby, S. (2009) *Examining Tuskegee: the infamous syphilis study and its legacy*, The John Hope Franklin series in African American history and culture, Chapel Hill, University of North Carolina Press.

Rowbotham, S. (1977) *Hidden from history: 300 years of women's oppression and the fight against it*, London, Pluto Press.

Rowley, J. (2010) 'Conducting Research Interviews', *Management Research Review*, vol. 35, no. 3/4, pp. 260–271.

Rutter, J. and Smith, G.W.H. (2005) 'Ethnographic Presence in a Nebulous Setting', in Hine, C. (ed.), *Virtual methods: issues in social research on the Internet*, Oxford, Berg, pp. 81–92.

Sarsby, J. (1984) 'The Fieldwork Experience', in Allen, R.F. (ed), *Ethnographic research: A Guide to General Conduct*, London, Academic Press.

Spicker, P. (2011) 'Ethical Covert Research', *Sociology*, vol. 45, no. 1, pp. 118–133.

Spivak, G.C. (1988) 'Subaltern Studies: Deconstructing Historiography', in Guha, R. (ed), *Selected Subaltern studies*, New York, Oxford University Press.

Stokes, D. and Bergin, R. (2006) 'Methodology or "methodolatry"? An evaluation of focus groups and depth interviews', *Qualitative Market Research: An International Journal*, vol. 9, no. 1, pp. 26–37.

Taylor, P., Warhurst, C., Thompson, P. and Scholarios, D. (2009) 'On the Front Line', *Work, Employment & Society*, vol. 23, no. 1, pp. 7–11.

Thompson, E.P. (1991) *The Making of the English Working Class*, London, Penguin.

UK Data Service (2022) *About* [Online]. Available at https://ukdataservice.ac.uk/ (Accessed 18 August 2022).

Van Maanen, J. and Kolb, D. (1985) 'The professional apprentice: observations on fieldwork role in two organizational settings', *Research in the Sociology of Organizations*, vol. 4, pp. 1–33.

Webb, G., Haiven, M. and Benivolski, X. (2021) 'From the Belly of the Beast: Amazon workers, sci-fi and the space between utopia and disaster', *The Sociological Review Magazine* [Online]. Available at https://thesociologicalreview.org/magazine/november-2021/methods-and-methodology/from-the-belly-of-the-beast/.

Woodcock, J. (2017) *Working the Phones: Control and Resistance in Call Centres*, London, Pluto.

Woodcock, J. (2021) 'Workers Inquiry and the Experience of Work: Using Ethnographic Accounts of the Gig Economy', in Aroles, J., Vaujany, F.-X. and Dale, K. (eds), *Experiencing the New World of Work*, Cambridge, Cambridge University Press, pp. 136–156.

CHAPTER 6

FUTURE(S) OF EMPLOYMENT

The aim of this book was to provide resources for you to think critically and in more detail about our own experiences of work and debates on employment. It has introduced a series of critical approaches for understanding employment, trying to take people's experiences as a starting point. For this final chapter, we will briefly consider how employment might change in the future, particularly thinking about the themes and topics that have been discussed so far.

In chapter one, we discussed the history of employment from a critical perspective. We are now a long way from those early beginnings of work and relations have changed many times in the formation of contemporary employment. One of the important lessons that we can take from this history is that work was central to the formation of capitalism. Employment is not going anywhere anytime soon. We can see how Taylor's principles of scientific management are continuing to be developed, particularly through new forms of algorithmic management. Labour process theory provides tools that can be adapted today to make sense of the new kinds of employment relations that people find themselves in.

Throughout chapter two, we saw how the global divisions of labour have changed over time. If one thing is for certain about the future of work, it is that these division will continue to change and shift from one country to another. There is an ongoing search for a new 'spatial fix' (Harvey, 2006, 200), something that will only continue as imperialism develops. Looking back at the history of exploitation and extraction can help us make sense of these processes today. However, moving forward the climate crisis adds an existential threat to these dynamics. The role of employment – or more accurately employers – in pushing practices and policies that have relied on externalising the cost of economic growth on to the planet are now coming back.

In chapter three, we examined how employment is managed. The history of management has highlighted a crucial feature of employment that sets it apart from other activities: that we do it under the attempted control of management. The history of management is one of trying to find new approaches and techniques of control, that have spread throughout the employment relationship. There will continue to be new forms of technological control applied to the labour process, as management tries – once again – to find ways to overcome the practical challenges of planning, organising, commanding, coordinating, and controlling work. Resistance to this has been a feature of work historically and that will continue – as well as other approaches to organising work.

Chapter four introduced a series of current debates and dynamics on employment. Many of these are closely connected to the future of work. First, the state continues to have the power to shape employment, both for the better and the worse. Although the state has remained relatively absent from the debates or interventions on the future of work, through pressure from either above or below, this could change. Second, changes in the public sector have the potential to rapidly change both employment as well as the conditions in which many people work. The current trend is for the reduction of public sector employment, however, this is a political choice rather than a necessary trend. Third, post-industrial employment, particularly service work, has come to dominate many economies since the 1980s. If there is one constant about employment, it is that it changes. We are therefore likely to see new areas of employment expand while others contract, bring new post-this or post-that dynamics into play. Fourth, emotional and affective labour has become a much bigger part of the labour process, valued across a range of activities. However,

DOI: 10.4324/9781003279907-7

with further automation and pressures on employment, this kind of service could become more a premium service. Fifth, the subjective experiences of employment are becoming more precarious, even if this is not objectively matched in the statistics. Perhaps changes will make people feel more secure in their work, however, given the reach of precarity into much of contemporary employment, it is likely that this insecurity and instability will continue. Sixth, the debates on platforms and the gig economy are currently seen as one of the key changes taking place in the contemporary world of work. However, the employment model is being challenged in many jurisdictions and there are concerns about the medium- and longer-term profitability of this model. Perhaps more occupations will become Uberised – on the other hand this model may fall back. This does not, however, mean that technologies and techniques developed in the gig economy cannot be applied more widely. Finally, the current moment is a watershed moment for the trade union movement. There are the highest levels of strikes and worker organising that have been seen in many years. The direction that this develops in has the potential to reshape employment relations, changing the experiences and conditions under which many people work.

Chapter five focused on research methods for employment. It is here that the questions about the possible futures of work can be most productively posed. Each of us has an experience of how work and employment is changing. Through our practical experiences, as well as through using and adapting academic methods, we can start to build a picture of employment. This can both be about how it is changing, as well as how it could change. The most important thing you can do to understand the future of work is start that process.

THE DIFFERENT FUTURES OF WORK?

The main lesson of this book is that while employment may appear as a straightforward concept, in practice it is much more complicated. There are many forms of work (and things considered to be non-work) that are much broader than employment. Within employment there are a diversity of activities and ways of organising the relationship. The history of employment is filled with struggles over the form and content of employment and this has not changed today. It may be harder to see some of these struggles in particularly places or sectors, but that does not mean that they are not happening.

Many of the debates on the future of work focus on the role of technology and automation. For example, Maren Thomas Bannon, after speaking with venture capitalists, provided the following seven predictions:

1. Hybrid mix of in-office and at-home work will require a whole new software stack
2. Software automation will increasingly power everything from timekeeping to purchasing to logistics
3. Real-time, dynamic HR data infrastructure layers will transform workforce development
4. The great talent reshuffle will accelerate as 'office walls' continue coming down
5. Employers will increasingly focus on not just improving employee productivity, but also wellbeing
6. Tech tools will increasingly serve a wider range of workers, from small business owners to minorities to lower income workers
7. Future of work software will increasingly be built to facilitate human connection, rather than just efficiency

(Bannon, 2022)

Similarly, a McKinsey report gives the following context:

> The world of work is changing. Artificial intelligence and automation will make this shift as significant as the mechanization in prior generations of agriculture and manufacturing. While some jobs will be lost, and many others created, almost all will change. The COVID-19 crisis accelerated existing trends and caused organizations to reevaluate many aspects of work. This regularly updated collection of articles draws together our latest perspectives on the future of work, workforce, and workplace.
>
> (McKinsey & Company, 2022)

It is clear that there are significant changes on the horizon. However, these changes could go in many directions. What is often missing from these debates is that the future of work is not an imagined point on the horizon. Instead, the future of work is set by the choices made in the here and now. These changes are facilitated and constrained by the existing social relations and who has power. Many of the immediate changes are pointing employment in a negative direction. Each time one of these choices are made – to make workers redundant, to introduce electronic surveillance, to take away a benefit – we go one step further down the path to a dystopian future. So far, the evidence is that rapid technological automation is not bringing benefits to society more widely. What is needed is a positive vision of what this change could bring (Benanav, 2020).

The risk is that we focus too much on technology for considering the future of work and employment. The gig economy provides important lessons on why this is not enough:

> Technology alone has not brought about the gig economy, and there is nothing inevitable about its current or future state. For these reasons, it is important to not just reflect on what the gig economy is and where it comes from, but also to present a series of more desirable futures. More transparency and accountability, more worker-friendly regulation, greater structural power for workers, and the democratic ownership of platforms are all futures that help to build each other.
>
> (Woodcock and Graham, 2019, 141)

This means returning to the basic elements of employment: that it is a relationship between workers and employers. If we want to understand how to get to different kinds of employment, that means focusing on technology alone is not enough. We should start from the experience of employment and from workers' voice and actions. This can start charting another path to the future for employment that delivers for everyone.

ACADEMIC EXERCISES

Table 6.1 A Micro-Ethnography of Employment

For this activity you will do a short observation in a workplace. This could be somewhere you work, or another workplace that you have access to (for example, a customer-facing service workplace). Spending some time observing the workplace.

- Can you identify one element that is striking, surprising, unconventional, or unexpected in the workplace?
  - This could be something about the communication style (perhaps between workers, with customers, or the manager), work dress, workday habits, or something else.
- What do you notice when you write up the experience in a paragraph?
- How has this micro-ethnography changed your understanding of employment in that workplace context?

Table 6.2 Follow the Commodity

We do not often think about the different kinds of work that had to happen for us to buy
   something. Pick a commodity. It could be something like this book you are reading, a cup of
   coffee, or some other everyday commodity. Start by breaking down the different parts of the
   commodity. For example, this book needed to be written, copyedited, produced, printed, shipped,
   and sold in order for you to read it.

- Can you identify the different kinds of work that were needed to make the commodity?
- How are these different kinds of work connected?
- What can you find out about the conditions of the different jobs involved?
- How does thinking about this change your understanding of the commodity?

Table 6.3 Employment in Popular Culture

There are many representations of employment in popular culture, including in television, music,
   theatre, novels, and video games. For this task, you need to pick one example.

- What can this piece of culture tell us about work and employment?
- What effect does this representation have on how people might make sense of their work?
- What can you find out about the conditions of employment that were necessary to make this
   piece of culture?

Table 6.4 Explore Work Communities on Reddit

Many workers use social media like Reddit to connect with others in the same kind of employment.
   These communities can be a place to share knowledge about the work or ask for/provide advice.
   There are many of these communities on Reddit. For this activity you should pick a work
   community on Reddit and spend some time doing an online micro-ethnography.

- What sort of discussions about work are they having?
- Are you surprised by anything you have found in the community?
- What do you think workers are trying to get out of the community?
- What can this tell us about problems or challenges with the work?

Table 6.5 Interview Friends and Family about Their Employment

For this task, you should interview someone you already know about their employment. It could
   be a friend or a family member. Before the interview, think about what it is you already know
   about their employment. What else do you want to ask them? Prepare a short list of open-ended
   questions beforehand. Find the time to conduct the interview. Remember this should be a guided
   conversation and leave space for them to input into the direction. You can ask follow up questions
   or probe further on interesting topics.

- How did the interview go?
- Did you discover anything that you did not already know about their employment?
- What other things would be interesting to know that you couldn't find out from
   interviewing them?
- How would you do the interview differently if you did it again?

Table 6.6 Trade Unions and Employment

Trade unions have been an important part of many kinds of employment. Pick a kind of employment – this can be work you have done, want to do, or an area that interests you. Through desk research, try to answer the following questions.

- Is there a trade union that organises with these workers?
  - If yes, what does the trade union do? Has it had any recent successes or failures?
  - If no, why do you think there is no trade union? Is there something about the work that makes this difficult? Are there historical or other reasons why there is no trade union? Have there been any attempts at collective organising?
- Reflect on what you have learned about trade unions from this example. Has this changed anything about how you understand them?

Table 6.7 Social Media for Employment

The use of social media has become increasingly important for employment in many sectors and roles. In this two-part activity, you will consider how social media is used in this context.

First, conduct a social media audit of your own digital footprint. Imagine you are an employer deciding whether or not to hire you for a job.

- What sort of content do you find?
- Would this content make you more or less employable?
- After doing this yourself, how do you feel about the idea that an employer may investigate social media as part of the interviewing process?

Second, pick an industry or sector that you would like to work in (or want to understand better). Identify a key organisation and see what you can find by searching LinkedIn.

- What can you find out about an organisation by searching on LinkedIn?
- What sort of presentation or posts do individuals connected to the organisation choose to make public?
- How does this change your view of the sector or industry?

REFERENCES

Bannon, M.T. (2022) '7 Future Of Work Predictions For 2022', *Forbes* [Online]. Available at www.forbes.com/sites/marenbannon/2021/12/08/7-future-of-work-predictions-for-2022/.
Benanav, A. (2020) *Automation and the future of work*, London, Verso.
Harvey, D. (2006) *The Limits to Capital*, London, Verso.
McKinsey & Company (2022) *Future of Work* [Online]. Available at www.mckinsey.com/featured-insights/future-of-work.
Woodcock, J. and Graham, M. (2019) *The Gig Economy: A Critical Introduction*, Cambridge, Polity.

INDEX

Note: Page numbers in *italic* denote figures and in **bold** denote tables.

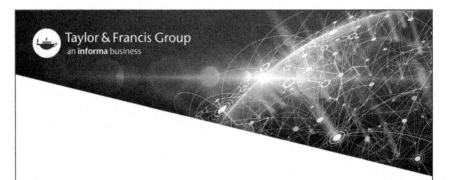

Printed in the United States
by Baker & Taylor Publisher Services